A
MEDITATIVE
COMMENTARY
ON THE
NEW TESTAMENT

MATTHEW: JESUS IS KING

MATTHEW: JESUS IS KING

by Gary Holloway

MATTHEW: JESUS IS KING
Published by Leafwood Publishers

Copyright 2005 by Gary Holloway

ISBN 0-9767790-1-3
Printed in the United States of America

Cover design by Greg Jackson, Jackson Design Co., llc

ALL RIGHTS RESERVED
No part of this publication may be reproduced, stored in a retrieval system, or transmitted in any form by any means—electronic, mechanical, photocopying, recording or otherwise—without prior written consent.

Scripture quotations, unless otherwise noted, are from *The Holy Bible, New International Version.* Copyright 1984, International Bible Society. Used by permission of Zondervan Publishers.

For information:
Leafwood Publishers
1409 Hunter Ridge
Siloam Springs, AR 72761
1-877-634-6004 (toll free)

Visit our website: www.leafwoodpublishers.com

05 06 07 08 09 10 / 7 6 5 4 3 2 1

To Carl McKelvey, my father in the faith

CONTENTS

INTRODUCTION:

9 .... HEARING GOD IN SCRIPTURE
17 .... THE SPIRITUALITY OF MATTHEW

MEDITATIONS:

21 .... GOD'S PEOPLE (MATTHEW 1:1-17)
27 .... A RIGHTEOUS MAN (MATTHEW 1:18-25)
31 .... THEY WORSHIPED HIM (MATTHEW 2:1-12)
36 .... DELIVERED FROM EVIL (MATTHEW 2:13-23)
40 .... TURN TO GOD (MATTHEW 3:1-17)
45 .... TEMPTATION (MATTHEW 4:1-11)
50 .... FOLLOW THE LIGHT (MATTHEW 4:12-25)
54 .... GOD AT WORK (MATTHEW 5:1-12)
58 .... HIGHER RIGHTEOUSNESS (MATTHEW 5:13-20)
62 .... INSIDE-OUT OBEDIENCE (MATTHEW 5:21-37)
67 .... PERFECT LOVE (MATTHEW 5:38-48)
71 .... SECRET RIGHTEOUSNESS (MATTHEW 6:1-18)
76 .... TREASURE (MATTHEW 6:19-34)
80 .... DO UNTO OTHERS (MATTHEW 7:1-12)
84 .... DOING THE WORD (MATTHEW 7:13-29)
90 .... ASTONISHED (MATTHEW 8:1-17)
94 .... FOLLOWING JESUS (MATTHEW 8:18-9:12)
99 .... CARING AND CURING (MATTHEW 9:14-34)

104 ......WORKERS (MATTHEW 9:35-10:42)

110 ......ELIJAH (MATTHEW 11:1-24)

115 ......SERVANT AND LORD (MATTHEW 11:25-12:50)

122 ......TRUE VALUE (MATTHEW 13:1-58)

129 ......DON'T BE AFRAID (MATTHEW 14:1-15:20)

136 ......BREAD (MATTHEW 15:21-16:12)

141 ......REVELATION (MATTHEW 16:13-17:23)

147 ......KINGDOM (MATTHEW 17:24-18:35)

154 ......DEMANDS AND REWARDS (MATTHEW 19:1-20:34)

162 ......AUTHORITY (MATTHEW 21:1-32)

168 ......INVITATION (MATTHEW 21:33-22:33)

175 ......HYPOCRITES (MATTHEW 22:34-23:39)

182 ......SIGNS (MATTHEW 24:1-51)

189 ......JUDGMENT (MATTHEW 25:1-46)

196 ......BETRAYAL (MATTHEW 26:1-46)

203 ......TRIAL (MATTHEW 26:47-27:26)

210 ......CROSS (MATTHEW 27:27-61)

216 ......RESURRECTION (MATTHEW 27:62-28:20)

INTRODUCTION:
HEARING GOD IN SCRIPTURE

There are many commentaries, guides, and workbooks on the various books of the Bible. How is this series different? It is not intended to answer all your scholarly questions about the Bible, or even make you an expert in the details of Scripture. Instead, this series is designed to help you hear the voice of God for your everyday life. It is a guide to meditation on the Bible, meditation that will allow the Bible to transform you.

We read in many ways. We might scan the newspaper for information, read a map for location, read a novel for pleasure, or read a textbook to pass a test. These are all good ways to read, depending on our circumstances.

A young soldier far away from home who receives a letter from his wife reads in yet another way. He might scan the letter quickly at first for news and information. But his longing for his beloved causes him to read the letter again and again, hearing her sweet voice in every line. He slowly treasures each word of this precious letter.

Bible Study

So also, there are many good ways to read the Bible, depending on our circumstances. Bible study is absolutely necessary for our life with God. We rightly study the Bible for information. We ask, "Who wrote this?" "When was it written?" "Who were the original readers?"

"How do these words apply to me?" More importantly, we want information about God. Who is he? What does he think of me? What does he want from me?

There is no substitute for this kind of close, dedicated Bible study. We must know what the Bible says to know our standing with God. We therefore read the Bible to discover true doctrine or teaching. But some in their emphasis on the authority and inspiration of the Bible have forgotten that Bible study is not an end in itself. We want to know God through Scripture. We want to have a relationship with the Teacher, not just the teachings.

Jesus tells some of God's people in his day, "You diligently study the Scriptures because you think that by them you possess eternal life. These are the Scriptures that testify about me, yet you refuse to come to me to have life" (John 5:39-40). He's not telling them to study their Bibles less, but he is reminding them of the deeper purpose of Bible study—to draw us to God through Jesus. Bible study is a means, not an end.

Yet the way many of us have learned to study the Bible may actually get in the way of hearing God. "Bible study" may sound a lot like schoolwork, and many of us were happy to get out of school. "Bible study" may call to mind pictures of intellectuals surrounded by books in Greek and Hebrew, pondering meanings too deep for ordinary people. The method of Bible study that has been popular for some time focuses on the strangeness of the Bible. It was written long ago, far away, and in languages we cannot read. There is a huge gap between us and the original readers of the Bible, a gap that can only be bridged by scholars, not by average folk.

There is some truth and some value in that "scholarly" method. It is true that the Bible was not written originally to us. Knowing ancient languages and customs can at times help us understand the Bible better. However, one unintended result of this approach is to make the Bible distant from the people of God. We may come to think that

INTRODUCTION

we can only hear God indirectly through Scripture, that his word must be filtered through scholars. We may even think that deep Bible study is a matter of mastering obscure information about the Bible.

Meditation

But we read the Bible for more than information. By studying it, we experience transformation, the mysterious process of God at work in us. Through his loving words, God is calling us to life with him. He is forming us into the image of his Son.

Reading the Bible is not like reading other books. We are not simply trying to learn information or master material. Instead, we want to stand under the authority of Scripture and let God master us. While we read the Bible, it reads us, opening the depths of our being to the overpowering love of God. "For the word of God is living and active. Sharper than any double-edged sword, it penetrates even to dividing soul and spirit, joints and marrow; it judges the thoughts and attitudes of the heart. Nothing in all creation is hidden from God's sight. Everything is uncovered and laid bare before the eyes of him to whom we must give account" (Hebrews 4:12-13).

Opening our hearts to the word of God is meditation. Although this way of reading the Bible may be new to some, it has a long heritage among God's people. The Psalmist joyously meditates on the words of God (Psalm 1:2; 39:3; 119:15, 23, 27, 48, 78, 97, 99, 148). Meditation is taking the words of Scripture to heart and letting them ask questions of us. It is slowing chewing over a text, listening closely, reading God's message of love to us over and over. This is not a simple, easy, or naïve reading of Scripture, but a process that takes time, dedication, and practice on our part.

There are many ways to meditate on the Bible. One is praying the Scriptures. Prayer and Bible study really cannot be separated. One way of praying the Bible is to make the words of a text your prayer. Obviously, the prayer texts of Scripture, especially the Psalms, lend themselves to this. "The Lord is my shepherd" has been the prayer of many hearts.

However, it is proper and helpful to turn the words of the Bible into prayers. Commands from God can become prayers. "You shall have no other gods before me" (Exodus 20:3) can be prayed, "Lord, keep me from anything that takes your place in my heart." Stories can be prayed. Jesus heals a man born blind (John 9), and so we pray, "Lord Jesus open my eyes to who you truly are." Even the promises of the Bible become prayers. "Never will I leave you; never will I forsake you" (Deuteronomy 31:6; Hebrews 13:5) becomes "God help me know that you promise that you are always with me and so live my life without fear."

Obviously, there are many helpful ways of hearing the voice of God in Scripture. Again, the purpose of Bible reading and study is not to know more about the Bible, much less to pride ourselves as experts on Scripture. Instead, we read to hear the voice of our Beloved. We listen for a word of God for us.

Holy Reading

This commentary reflects one ancient way of meditation and praying the Scriptures known as *lectio divina* or holy reading. This method assumes that God wants to speak to us directly in the Bible, that the passage we are reading is God's word to us right now. The writers of the New Testament read the Old Testament with this same conviction. They saw the words of the Bible speaking directly to their own situation. They read with humility and with prayer.

The first step along this way of holy reading is listening to the Bible. Choose a biblical text that is not too long. This commentary

INTRODUCTION

breaks Matthew into smaller sections. The purpose is to hear God's voice in your current situation, not to cover material or prepare lessons. Get into a comfortable position and maintain silence before God for several minutes. This prepares the heart to listen. Read slowly. Savor each word. Perhaps read aloud. Listen for a particular phrase that speaks to you. Ask God, "What are you trying to tell me today?"

The next step is to meditate on that particular phrase. That meditation may include slowly repeating the phrase that seems to be for you today. As you think deeply on it, you might even memorize it. Committing biblical passages to memory allows us to hold them in our hearts all day long. If you keep a journal, you might write the passage there. Let those words sink deeply into your heart.

Then pray those words back to God in your heart. Those words may call up visual images, smells, sounds, and feelings. Pay attention to what God is giving you in those words. Then respond in faith to what those words say to your heart. What do they call you to be and to do? Our humble response might take the form of praise, thanksgiving, joy, confession, or even cries of pain.

The final step in this "holy reading" is contemplation of God. The words from God that we receive deeply in our hearts lead us to him. Through these words, we experience union with the all-powerful God of love. Again, one should not separate Bible reading from prayer. The words of God in Scripture transport us into the very presence of God where we joyfully rest in his love.

What keeps reading the Bible this way from becoming merely our own desires read back into Scripture? How do we know it is God's voice we hear and not our own?

Two things. One is prayer. We are asking God to open our hearts, minds, and lives to him. We ask to hear his voice, not ours and not the voice of the world around us.

The second thing that keeps this from being an exercise in self-deception is to study the Bible in community. By praying over Scripture in a group, we hear God's word together. God speaks through the other members of our group. The wisdom he gives them keeps us from private, selfish, and unusual interpretations. They help us keep our own voices in check, as we desire to listen to God alone.

HOW TO USE THIS COMMENTARY

This commentary provides assistance in holy reading of the Bible. It gives structure to daily personal devotions, family meditation, small group Bible studies, and church classes.

Daily Devotional

Listening, meditation, prayer, contemplation. How does this commentary fit into this way of Bible study? Consider it as a conversation partner. We have taken a section of Scripture and then broken it down into four short daily readings. After listening, meditating, praying, and contemplating the passage for the day, use the questions suggested in the commentary to provoke deeper reflection. This provides a structure for a daily fifteen minute devotional four days a week. On the fifth day, read the entire passage, meditate, and then use the questions to reflect on the meaning of the whole. On day six, take our meditations on the passage as conversation with another who has prayed over the text.

If you want to begin daily Bible reading, but need guidance, this provides a Monday-Saturday experience that prepares the heart for worship and praise on Sunday. This structure also results in a communal reading of Scripture, instead of a private reading. Even if you use this commentary alone, you are not reading privately. God is at work in you and in the conversation you have with another (the author of the commentary) who has sought to hear God through this particular passage of the Bible.

Family Bible Study

This commentary can also provide an arrangement for family Bible study. Many Christian parents want to lead their children in daily study, but don't know where to begin or how to structure their time. Using the six-day plan outlined above means the entire family can read, meditate, pray, and reflect on the shorter passages, using the questions provided. On day five, they can review the entire passage, and then on day six, read the meditations in the commentary to prompt reflection and discussion. God will bless our families beyond our imaginations through the prayerful study of his word.

Weekly Group Study

This commentary can also structure small group Bible study. Each member of the group should have meditated over the daily readings and questions for the five days preceding the group meeting, using the method outlined above. The day before the group meeting, each member should read and reflect on the meditations in the commentary on that passage. You then can meet once a week to hear God's word together. In that group meeting, the method of holy reading would look something like this:

Listening
    1) Five minutes of silence.
    2) Slow reading of the biblical passage for that week.

3) A minute of silent meditation on the passage.

4) Briefly share with the group the word or phrase that struck you.

Personal Message

5) A second reading of the same passage.

6) A minute of silence.

7) Where does this touch your life today?

8) Responses: I hear, I see, etc.

Life Response

9) Brief silence.

10) What does God want you to do today in light of this word?

Group Prayer

11) Have each member of the group pray aloud for the person on his or her left, asking God to bless the word he has given them.

The procedure suggested here can be used in churches or in neighborhood Bible studies. Church members would use the daily readings Monday-Friday in their daily devotionals. This commentary intentionally provides no readings on the sixth day, so that we can spend Saturdays as a time of rest, not rest from Bible study, but a time to let God's word quietly work its way deep into our hearts. Sunday during Bible school or in home meetings, the group would meet to experience the weekly readings together, using the group method described above. It might be that the sermon for each Sunday could be on the passage for that week.

There are churches that have used this structure to great advantage. In the hallways of those church buildings, the talk is not of the local football team or the weather, but of the shared experience of the Word of God for that week.

And that is the purpose of our personal and communal study, to

INTRODUCTION

hear the voice of God, our loving Father who wants us to love him in return. He deeply desires a personal relationship with us. Father, Son, and Spirit make a home inside us (see John 14:16-17, 23). Our loving God speaks to his children! But we must listen for his voice. That listening is not a matter of gritting our teeth and trying harder to hear. Instead, it is part of our entire life with God. That is what Bible study is all about.

Through daily personal prayer and meditation on God's word and through a communal reading of Scripture, our most important conversation partner, the Holy Spirit, will do his mysterious and marvelous work. Among other things, the Spirit pours God's love into our hearts (Romans 5:5), bears witness to our spirits that we are God's children (Romans 8:16), intercedes for us with God (Romans 8:26), and enlightens us as to God's will (Ephesians 1:17).

So this is an invitation to personal daily Bible study, to praying the Scriptures, to sharing with fellow believers, to hear the voice of God. God will bless us, our families, our churches, and his world if we take the time to be still, listen, and do his word.

THE SPIRITUALITY OF MATTHEW

Matthew is a gospel, a telling of the good news of Jesus. Like the other gospels in the New Testament, Matthew tells the story of Jesus from a particular perspective, emphasizing some things about Jesus more than others. The purpose of Matthew and the other gospels is not just to give us historical information about Jesus, but to call us to faith in him. Through the words of Matthew, the Holy Spirit works, creating faith in our hearts and transforming us into the image of Jesus, the Son of God.

Matthew particularly emphasizes Jesus as the great King who

rules over his kingdom. Jesus is descended from King David (Matthew 1:6). When he is born, Magi from the east come to bring gifts to him as the king of the Jews (Matthew 2:1-12). Both John the Baptist and Jesus proclaim that the kingdom of heaven is near (Matthew 3:3; 4:17). Jesus shows his authority as king in his teaching and in his miracles. Even the charge against Jesus at his crucifixion reads, "This Is Jesus, The King of the Jews" (Matthew 27:37).

But few of us know what it's like to live under a king. We once had a king in America and we got rid of him. So as we meditatively read Matthew for spiritual growth, we must ask certain questions. What kind of king is this Jesus? How do we treat him as king? What does it mean to live in his kingdom? These are the questions Matthew answers.

Prophet and King

In addition to calling Jesus king, Matthew refers to him as a prophet (Matthew 13:57; 16:14; 21:11, 46). Jesus is the authoritative interpreter of the Law. Like Moses, he speaks from a mountain and claims to fulfill the Law and the Prophets. As we read Matthew, we must open our hearts to the astounding words of Jesus, words that reveal the intent of God in the Law. Unlike the Pharisees, Jesus does not see the Law as harsh but as a mirror into the heart of a loving God.

The Kingdom of Love

Indeed, love is at the center of the Law. When asked the greatest commandment, Jesus replied: " 'Love the Lord your God with all your heart and with all your soul and with all your mind.' This is the first and greatest commandment. And the second is like it: 'Love your neighbor as yourself.' All the Law and the Prophets hang on these two commandments" (Matthew 22:37-40).

Twice in Matthew, at the baptism of Jesus and at the transfiguration, a voice from heaven proclaims about Jesus, "This is my Son, whom I love." Jesus is not the only beloved child of God. All who enter the heavenly kingdom are beloved daughters and sons of God. Living in his kingdom of love, we show God's love to our neighbors. This love for neighbor includes love for enemies and persecutors (Matthew 5:43-44). God rules in love, sending blessings on both good and bad. To live in God's kingdom is to embody that perfect love of the Father (Matthew 5:45-48).

A Kingdom of the Heart

The place where God rules is in our hearts, the center of our very beings. "Heart" in Matthew is more than emotions; it includes those sincere actions that spring from the core of who we are. As we saw above, we are to love God with all our hearts. Jesus condemns the Pharisees and teachers of his day for trying to follow God outwardly when their hearts are far from him (Matthew 15:8). Both evil actions and good ones find their source in the heart (see Matthew 5:28, 12:34, 15:18-19, 18:35). To live in the kingdom requires purity of heart (Matthew 5:8). Rejecting Jesus as king comes from a hard and calloused heart (Matthew 13:15-19).

Life in the Kingdom

Making Jesus our king brings life. But living in the kingdom is demanding. The road to life is narrow and difficult (Matthew 7:13-14). Kingdom living means not just hearing the words of Jesus but doing them (Matthew 7:21-27). Since Jesus himself embodies the kingdom, following him means living as he lives—completely dependent on our Father but with no place of our own to lay our heads (Matthew 6:33; 8:19-20). It means facing persecution from your own family because of their hatred of Jesus (Matthew 10:21-23). It means serving others instead of wanting to rule (Matthew 23:11). It means drinking the cup of suffering (Matthew 20:23).

If Jesus truly is our king, then we must recognize his authority, not only the authority shown in his teaching and miracles, but that all authority is his after the resurrection.

Kingdom as Community

But we never live in the kingdom alone. The kingdom Jesus announces is a community of faith. We are disciples together. Indeed, Matthew is the only gospel that uses the word church. Jesus promises to build the church on believers like Peter, saying the gates of hades will not overcome it (Matthew 16:18). He even gives instruction on what to do as church if others sin against us (Matthew 18:15-20). As disciples of King Jesus, we are bound together in love. The last command from our king in Matthew is to go make other disciples, knowing that our Lord is ever with us.

Kingdom Spirituality

So as we read and meditate on Matthew, let us open our hearts and lives to the possibilities of living in the kingdom of God. Making Jesus our king is a daily discipleship, following him wherever he leads. If we take Matthew seriously, we might (like his original hearers) be shocked by the words of Jesus, astonished by his power, and overwhelmed at his compassion. He asks us loyally to follow him in trust.

MEDITATIONS

GOD'S PEOPLE
(MATTHEW 1:1-17)

Day One Reading and Questions:

¹A record of the genealogy of Jesus Christ the son of David, the son of Abraham:
²Abraham was the father of Isaac,
  Isaac the father of Jacob,
  Jacob the father of Judah and his brothers,

1) Have you done research into your family tree? Why or why not? What motivates people to research their genealogies?

2) Go back to Genesis and read the story of Abraham. What were the turning points in his relationship with God?

3) Look again at the story of Jacob. How was he an unlikely person for God to bless?

Day Two Reading and Questions:

³Judah the father of Perez and Zerah, whose mother was Tamar,

Perez the father of Hezron,
Hezron the father of Ram,
⁴Ram the father of Amminadab,
Amminadab the father of Nahshon,
Nahshon the father of Salmon,
⁵Salmon the father of Boaz, whose mother was Rahab,
Boaz the father of Obed, whose mother was Ruth,
Obed the father of Jesse,
⁶and Jesse the father of King David.

1) Read the Tamar story (Genesis 38). Why did Tamar do what she did with Judah? Was she right to do so? Is it surprising to find her in the family tree of Jesus?

2) Do the same with Rahab (Joshua 2; 6:22-23). Again, is she the kind of ancestor you would be proud of? Why or why not?

3) Finally, look at the story of Ruth. What do all three of these women have in common? What does that tell us about God's work among us?

Day Three Reading and Questions:

David was the father of Solomon, whose mother had been Uriah's wife,

1) Recount all the stories you know about David. What do they have in common?

2) Read the story of Uriah and David (2 Samuel 11). How can you explain what David did? What lesson is there for us here? Again, why does Matthew bring up such an embarrassing story in the family of Jesus?

Day Four Reading and Questions:

⁷Solomon the father of Rehoboam,
  Rehoboam the father of Abijah,
  Abijah the father of Asa,
  ⁸Asa the father of Jehoshaphat,
  Jehoshaphat the father of Jehoram,
  Jehoram the father of Uzziah,
  ⁹Uzziah the father of Jotham,
  Jotham the father of Ahaz,
  Ahaz the father of Hezekiah,
  ¹⁰Hezekiah the father of Manasseh,
  Manasseh the father of Amon,
  Amon the father of Josiah,

1) What comes to mind when you hear the name "Solomon"? Was Solomon a good king or a bad one? Was he faithful to God?

2) Go to Kings and Chronicles and look at the life of one of the kings after Solomon on this list. Was that king faithful to God? If not, why is he in the family line of Jesus?

3) Look at the reign of Josiah (2 Kings 23). What significant things did he do to turn people back to the Lord? What are some similarities between Josiah and Jesus?

Day Five Reading and Questions:

¹¹and Josiah the father of Jeconiah and his brothers at the time of the exile to Babylon.

¹²After the exile to Babylon:

Jeconiah was the father of Shealtiel,

Shealtiel the father of Zerubbabel,

¹³Zerubbabel the father of Abiud,

Abiud the father of Eliakim,

Eliakim the father of Azor,

¹⁴Azor the father of Zadok,

Zadok the father of Akim,

Akim the father of Eliud,

¹⁵Eliud the father of Eleazar,

Eleazar the father of Matthan,

Matthan the father of Jacob,

¹⁶and Jacob the father of Joseph, the husband of Mary, of whom was born Jesus, who is called Christ.

¹⁷Thus there were fourteen generations in all from Abraham to David, fourteen from David to the exile to Babylon, and fourteen from the exile to the Christ.

> 1) Think about the concept of exile. What would it feel like to be exiled? Why did God exile his people? Why did he bring them back home? What does the story of Jesus have to do with exile?
>
> 2) Read back over this entire list of names. Why do you think Matthew begins his Gospel this way? Is it the way you would begin the story of Jesus?
>
> 3) What person on this list do you feel most similar to yourself? Why do you relate to him or her?

MEDITATIONS ON MATTHEW 1:1-17

What a way to start a book! A list of names!

It's not the way a contemporary writer would begin a book. We see a long list of hard to pronounce names and automatically skip to the next section.

But these are not just names. They are people. Flesh and blood people who had the same struggles, the same joys, the same boredom, and the same faith as we.

These are our people. Abraham, who left a comfortable and familiar home to go God knows where. And only God knew where, not Abraham. Yet Abraham goes. Abraham who receives a miracle from God, a child born in his old age. A child, Isaac, that God later demands in sacrifice. And Abraham, takes his beloved son, builds the altar, and raises the knife—all the while trusting that God will provide his own sacrifice.

Then there are the women. All outsiders. All oppressed. Tamar who has to pretend to be a prostitute to get justice from her father-in-law, Judah. Rahab, who is a prostitute and a foreigner. Ruth, a foreigner who must rely on an Israelite man to "redeem" her.

And David. Singer, soldier, hero, king. A man after God's own heart who becomes an adulterer and murderer. But he knows how to plead for mercy. And he knows how to show it.

Then those in exile. Strangers. Homeless. Away from the land of promise. No temple. No priesthood. No hope? Yes! Hope in the Lord. Hope for restoration. No matter how low God's people fall, he is there to lift them up.

What a way to start a book! These are our people. What's more, they are Jesus' people. In this list, Matthew captures all of human history. All of what has gone before, all that now has come in Jesus. Abraham, willing to follow God no matter what the cost. His son,

Jesus, willing to follow, even though he will be the sacrifice God supplies. Women that the world has marginalized, heroically claiming their place in God's kingdom. Jesus, rejected by the world, but the king of the universe. David, a man after God's own heart. Jesus, God's own heart, who shows mercy to his greatest enemies. Exiles, far away from home. Jesus, himself an exile in his own hometown, who shows us the way home.

What a way to start a gospel!

"Father of Abraham, Tamar, Rahab, and David, Father of our Lord Jesus Christ, this day remind us of those who have gone before us in faith. May we follow in their steps. Lord Jesus, in you are all the hopes of the world."

MEDITATIONS

A RIGHTEOUS MAN
(MATTHEW 1:18-25)

Day One Reading and Questions:

[18]This is how the birth of Jesus Christ came about: His mother Mary was pledged to be married to Joseph, but before they came together, she was found to be with child through the Holy Spirit. [19]Because Joseph her husband was a righteous man and did not want to expose her to public disgrace, he had in mind to divorce her quietly.

1) Imagine what Joseph's feelings must have been when he found out Mary was pregnant. What would you have thought if you were in his shoes?

2) What does it mean that Mary was with child through the Holy Spirit? What does that tell us about the work of the Spirit?

3) What is the relationship between being a righteous man and not wanting to publicly disgrace Mary? Does true righteousness always include mercy?

Day Two Reading and Questions:

[20]But after he had considered this, an angel of the Lord appeared to him in a dream and said, "Joseph son of David, do not be afraid to take Mary home as your wife, because what is conceived in her is from

the Holy Spirit. ²¹She will give birth to a son, and you are to give him the name Jesus, because he will save his people from their sins."

> 1) Why would Joseph be afraid to take Mary as his wife? Is fear the emotion you would have expected here?
>
> 2) Why is Joseph called "son of David" here? How is he like David?
>
> 3) The name Jesus is the same as the name Joshua, meaning "The Lord saves." How is Jesus like Joshua?

Day Three Reading and Questions:

²²All this took place to fulfill what the Lord had said through the prophet: ²³"The virgin will be with child and will give birth to a son, and they will call him Immanuel"—which means, "God with us."

> 1) Reread the verse quoted here (Isaiah 7:14) in its original context. What was God promising in Isaiah? How is that promise fulfilled here?
>
> 2) What do we mean when we call Jesus, "God with us?" Hasn't God always been with his people?
>
> 3) Does everyone call Jesus, "Immanuel—God with us?" What does it take to call him this and really mean it?

Day Four Reading and Questions:

²⁴When Joseph woke up, he did what the angel of the Lord had commanded him and took Mary home as his wife. ²⁵But he had no

union with her until she gave birth to a son. And he gave him the name Jesus.

1) How did Joseph know this was more than just a strange dream? Does God still speak in dreams? If so, how do we know he is speaking?

2) Do angels still help God's people today? How?

3) It is Joseph who names the baby "Jesus." Is there something precious about that name? How is that name used and misused today?

Day Five Reading and Questions:

Go back and read the entire passage.

1) What does this passage tell us about the character of Joseph? What words would you use to describe him?

2) Do you think we place enough emphasis on Joseph. Why or why not?

3) This passage may seem far removed from our own experience. Think of some ways you can relate to Joseph. What are some times in your life when you were afraid of hurting and being hurt by someone you love?

MEDITATIONS ON MATTHEW 1:18-25

"She was found to be with child."

How perplexing those words must have been to Joseph. He loved Mary. He knew she loved him. They had solemnly pledged themselves to one another. Joseph knew that Mary was a good woman, a righteous woman, a woman who kept her vows.

But the stubborn fact remained. "She was found to be with child." It made no sense to Joseph. Confused, hurt, and stunned, all he could think to do was to quietly separate from Mary. Still, it made no sense. "She was found to be with child."

It took a miracle from God to make sense of it all. The angel comes in a dream and says, "Do not be afraid." What fear did Joseph have? His fear is our greatest fear. Fear of rejection. Fear that those we love the most have betrayed us. Fear that all our plans have come crashing down. Fear of hurting and being hurt.

"Do not be afraid." Easier said than done. We rightly honor Mary for her overwhelming trust and obedience. What about Joseph? What kind of trust does it take to believe, "what is conceived in her is from the Holy Spirit?" Yet Joseph believes and acts. He is no longer afraid. He takes Mary as his wife. Fear turns to joy. Faith leads to salvation. "God with us." Mary gives birth to Jesus, meaning, "the Lord saves."

What about our fears? What words make us afraid? "She is with child." "He's found someone else." "The tests came back positive." "Your son has been arrested." "Your mother has Alzheimer's."

Fear of hurting and being hurt. Do we, like Joseph, trust a God who speaks in dreams? Can we believe words that sound too good to believe? Do not be afraid. This is from the Holy Spirit. God is with us. He will save his people.

"Father, you know our hearts, our hurts, and our fears. Give us faith, like Joseph, to believe the good news and obey it. May we this day live the news that you are with us, that what happens to us is from your Spirit, and that you are with us always in Jesus."

THEY WORSHIPED HIM
(MATTHEW 2:1-12)

DAY ONE READING AND QUESTIONS:

¹After Jesus was born in Bethlehem in Judea, during the time of King Herod, Magi from the east came to Jerusalem ²and asked, "Where is the one who has been born king of the Jews? We saw his star in the east and have come to worship him."

1) What do you know about Herod the Great? Look him up in a Bible dictionary or on the web. How would you describe his character?

2) Also look up Magi. Who were they? How do we usually see them portrayed in the Christmas story? Is this accurate? Why do they follow stars?

3) In what sense is Jesus, "king of the Jews?" Is he a king like Herod?

DAY TWO READING AND QUESTIONS:

³When King Herod heard this he was disturbed, and all Jerusalem with him. ⁴When he had called together all the people's chief priests and teachers of the law, he asked them where the Christ was to be born. ⁵"In Bethlehem in Judea," they replied, "for this is what the prophet has written:

⁶ 'But you, Bethlehem, in the land of Judah,

are by no means least among the rulers of Judah;
   for out of you will come a ruler
who will be the shepherd of my people Israel.' "

1) Why is Herod disturbed when he heard this? Is there a foreshadowing here of how later rulers will feel about Jesus?

2) Jesus here is called "the Christ." Look up "Christ" or "Messiah." What does the word mean? Is this a name or a description?

3) In what sense is a ruler a shepherd? What does this say about the type of rule God expects from those who lead his people?

Day Three Reading and Questions:

[7]Then Herod called the Magi secretly and found out from them the exact time the star had appeared. [8]He sent them to Bethlehem and said, "Go and make a careful search for the child. As soon as you find him, report to me, so that I too may go and worship him."

1) Why does Herod call the Magi secretly? What comes to mind when you think about government secrets? Would you trust Herod? Do you trust the government?

2) Why does Herod want a "careful" search for the child? Is he sure the Magi will find the child? Is he convinced the Messiah has come? Why does he say "the child," instead of "the Christ?"

3) Does Herod genuinely want to worship the child? Will there be others that claim to worship Jesus when they want to harm them? Who?

Day Four Reading and Questions:

⁹After they had heard the king, they went on their way, and the star they had seen in the east went ahead of them until it stopped over the place where the child was. ¹⁰When they saw the star, they were overjoyed. ¹¹On coming to the house, they saw the child with his mother Mary, and they bowed down and worshiped him. Then they opened their treasures and presented him with gifts of gold and of incense and of myrrh. ¹²And having been warned in a dream not to go back to Herod, they returned to their country by another route.

1) Why were the Magi overjoyed to see the star stop? Do we react to Jesus with the same joy?

2) Bowing before a king is expected, but the Magi also worship Jesus. What does this tell us about the depth of their faith? What does it tell us about the kingdom of Jesus?

3) They open their treasures and give to Jesus. What treasures do we bring to Jesus?

Day Five Reading and Questions:

Go back and read the entire passage.

1) What comes to mind when you hear "king?" How do we picture kings?

2) How does Jesus look like an unlikely king in this passage? What does that tell us about his kingdom?

3) Who or what really rules your life? Whom do you follow? To whom do you give your treasure?

MEDITATIONS ON MATTHEW 2:1-12.

Who is the king?

Jesus is born in the time of King Herod. But Magi, perhaps kings themselves, come looking for another, "the one who has been born king of the Jews."

Led by a star, they find their king. In joy they bow, worship, and give gifts to their king.

Herod also looks for the king. He asks the Magi to report to him immediately when they find the king, for he too wants to worship him. Herod lies. He knows that he alone is king of the Jews. Or does he know? Is he not afraid of this new rival, this new king? Herod wants to destroy, not to worship.

Who is our king? For Americans, the answer is easy. We had a king once and got rid of him. We have no king. We have a President, but our government is (in the words of Lincoln) "of the people, by the people, and for the people."

Still the question persists, "Who is our king?" Even in a democracy, the powers that be claim to be our rulers, our kings. Oh yes, they allow the free exercise of religion in its place, a place of private and personal devotion. Sometimes the powers even claim to bow the knee and worship Jesus, or at least to be "under God." But when the choice comes of who will actually control our lives, too often the powers—government, job, family, and the approval of others—are our true kings.

Who is our king? Not Herod, not the president, but if we are honest we might say, "I rule my own life." After all self-determination is a fundamental human right.

But no. The Magi or wise men are right. There is one king. To him we bow. To him we bring our treasures. Letting go of self-rule is painful. Admitting we are not the king is difficult (just ask Herod). But if we worship Jesus, like the Magi, we find true joy.

"King Jesus, rule our lives. May no power, not even our own wills, keep us from the joy of worshipping you."

DELIVERED FROM EVIL

(MATTHEW 2:13-23)

Day One Reading and Questions:

¹³When they had gone, an angel of the Lord appeared to Joseph in a dream. "Get up," he said, "take the child and his mother and escape to Egypt. Stay there until I tell you, for Herod is going to search for the child to kill him."

1) *Israel escaped famine by moving to Egypt under another Joseph (see Genesis 46:1-4). How is this story similar?*

2) *How had God provided money for this extended stay in Egypt? Does God often provide for us in unusual ways? Give examples from your own life.*

3) *Why is Herod trying to kill the child? Who else will try to kill him? Why?*

Day Two Reading and Questions:

¹⁴So he got up, took the child and his mother during the night and left for Egypt, ¹⁵where he stayed until the death of Herod. And so was fulfilled what the Lord had said through the prophet: "Out of Egypt I called my son."

1) *What does this story tell us about Joseph?*

2) *Is God at work in the death of Herod? What does this tell us about who really reigns?*

3) *God saves Israel from famine by sending them to Egypt. Later he saves them from slavery by bringing them out of Egypt. What are some other parallels between Jesus and the story of Israel? In what ways does Jesus embody Israel?*

Day Three Reading and Questions:

[16] When Herod realized that he had been outwitted by the Magi, he was furious, and he gave orders to kill all the boys in Bethlehem and its vicinity who were two years old and under, in accordance with the time he had learned from the Magi. [17] Then what was said through the prophet Jeremiah was fulfilled:

[18] "A voice is heard in Ramah,
    weeping and great mourning,
Rachel weeping for her children
    and refusing to be comforted,
because they are no more."

1) *It is hard to imagine the horror of what Herod does. What are some other massacres in history that shock us?*

2) *These innocent children suffer because Jesus is born in their town. Why does God allow such suffering? Does suffering always accompany the coming of Jesus? Why?*

3) *Rachel refuses to be comforted. Have you suffered a grief that refuses comfort?*

Day Four Reading and Questions:

[19]After Herod died, an angel of the Lord appeared in a dream to Joseph in Egypt [20]and said, "Get up, take the child and his mother and go to the land of Israel, for those who were trying to take the child's life are dead."

[21]So he got up, took the child and his mother and went to the land of Israel. [22]But when he heard that Archelaus was reigning in Judea in place of his father Herod, he was afraid to go there. Having been warned in a dream, he withdrew to the district of Galilee, [23]and he went and lived in a town called Nazareth. So was fulfilled what was said through the prophets: "He will be called a Nazarene."

1) Should Joseph have been afraid of Archelaus? Didn't the angel tell him earlier not to be afraid? Is there a proper time for caution or fear?

2) How does God always speak to Joseph? Does that remind you of another Joseph? What other similarities can you find between these two Josephs?

3) What reputation did Galilee and Nazareth have? Why didn't God have Jesus grow up in the great city of Jerusalem?

Day Five Reading and Questions:

Go back and read the entire passage.

1) What comes to mind when you think of Egypt? What part does Egypt play in the story of Israel? What part does it play in the story of Jesus?

2) In what ways has God brought us out of Egypt? How is the story of Israel and the story here of Jesus our story too?

3) Who really has the power here, Herod or God? How does each of them show their power? What does that tell us about God's power in our lives today?

MEDITATIONS ON MATTHEW 2:13-23

"Out of Egypt I have called my son."
When a Pharaoh came to power who did not know Joseph, he enslaved the Israelites. Only the powerful hand of God through Moses delivered his people, calling them from bondage in Egypt to freedom in the Promised Land.

When Herod hears the Magi have left without telling him the identity of this new king, he takes action. To be on the safe side, he has every male child in Bethlehem under two years old killed. But the powerful hand of God protects his Son, sending him into Egypt and bringing him out again when Herod is dead.

When we decide that Jesus is our king, the powers that be respond with slavery and death. But who truly is the king? Who truly has the power? It is God who delivers. He delivers his son Israel from Egypt. He delivers his Son Jesus from Herod.

Whom do we trust to deliver us from evil? The government? Homeland Security? Our health insurance policy? Our investment firm? Terror and terrorists are nothing new. What can be more terrible than slaughtering innocent children? But God delivered Jesus. He delivered Israel. He will deliver us.

"Father, increase our trust in you. No matter what horrors may await us this day, may we rest secure in your care for us as your children."

TURN TO GOD

(MATTHEW 3:1-17)

Day One Reading and Questions:

¹In those days John the Baptist came, preaching in the Desert of Judea ²and saying, "Repent, for the kingdom of heaven is near." ³This is he who was spoken of through the prophet Isaiah:

"A voice of one calling in the desert,
'Prepare the way for the Lord,
    make straight paths for him.' "

⁴John's clothes were made of camel's hair, and he had a leather belt around his waist. His food was locusts and wild honey. ⁵People went out to him from Jerusalem and all Judea and the whole region of the Jordan. ⁶Confessing their sins, they were baptized by him in the Jordan River.

1) What comes to mind when you hear the word, "repent?" What does repentance look like?

2) What is meant by "the kingdom of heaven?" In what sense was the kingdom near? What is the relationship between repentance and the nearness of the kingdom of heaven?

3) What is the relationship among repentance, confession, and baptism?

Day Two Reading and Questions:

⁷But when he saw many of the Pharisees and Sadducees coming to where he was baptizing, he said to them: "You brood of vipers! Who warned you to flee from the coming wrath? ⁸Produce fruit in keeping with repentance. ⁹And do not think you can say to yourselves, 'We have Abraham as our father.' I tell you that out of these stones God can raise up children for Abraham. ¹⁰The ax is already at the root of the trees, and every tree that does not produce good fruit will be cut down and thrown into the fire.

1) Why is John so harsh toward the Pharisees and Sadducees? Doesn't he want them to be converted? What implications might this have toward evangelism today?

2) Matthew begins with an emphasis on Abraham as an ancestor of Jesus. Here John does not seem to think much of having Abraham as an ancestor. What does it mean to be descended from Abraham?

3) What is the good fruit that John calls for?

Day Three Reading and Questions:

¹¹"I baptize you with water for repentance. But after me will come one who is more powerful than I, whose sandals I am not fit to carry. He will baptize you with the Holy Spirit and with fire. ¹²His winnowing fork is in his hand, and he will clear his threshing floor, gathering his wheat into the barn and burning up the chaff with unquenchable fire."

1) What does it mean to be baptized for repentance? How does this relate to John's warning to the Pharisees and Sadducees?

2) What does John mean by baptizing with the Holy Spirit? When will Jesus do this?

3) What does John mean by baptizing with fire? When will Jesus do this?

Day Four Reading and Questions:

[13] Then Jesus came from Galilee to the Jordan to be baptized by John. [14] But John tried to deter him, saying, "I need to be baptized by you, and do you come to me?"
[15] Jesus replied, "Let it be so now; it is proper for us to do this to fulfill all righteousness." Then John consented.
[16] As soon as Jesus was baptized, he went up out of the water. At that moment heaven was opened, and he saw the Spirit of God descending like a dove and lighting on him. [17] And a voice from heaven said, "This is my Son, whom I love; with him I am well pleased."

1) Why is Jesus baptized? Did he need to repent? What does it mean to fulfill all righteousness? How does Jesus become righteousness for us (see 2 Corinthians 5:21)?

2) What three things happened to Jesus at his baptism? What happened to us at our baptisms?

3) In what other ways are our baptisms like that of Jesus?

Day Five Reading and Questions:

Go back and read the entire passage.

1) Why is repentance so difficult? What does it take to truly repent?

2) What is the significance of baptism? What does it accomplish? What does it symbolize? What does God do in baptism?

3) Why does Jesus begin his ministry this way? What is the relationship between his ministry and John's? How are they similar? How are they different?

MEDITATIONS ON MATTHEW 3:1-17

    Surely, John wanted people to be baptized. His message was one of hope, "prepare the way of the Lord." The kingdom of heaven is near. It was good news.

    But it doesn't sound like good news. "Repent" he says. And when some come to repent, he calls them a bunch of snakes. Repentance may sound easy. Just turn back to God. But turning to God means turning away from all that we have known, turning from our identity as children of Abraham, or as good Americans, or (perhaps) even as good Christians. There must be fruit in keeping with repentance. Changed hearts. Changed lives. And change is painful.

    We want to hear the good news on our own terms. We want to give ourselves to Jesus, as long as it's not too demanding. But repentance and baptism demands all that we are. Jesus baptizes with the Holy Spirit, he demands to live in us. He baptizes with fire, fire that painfully purifies those who let it, but that destroys those who resist.

That's why John is so reluctant to baptize Jesus. Jesus has no need to turn back to God. But Jesus is baptized for our sins. To fulfill all righteousness. "God made him who had no sin to be sin for us, so that in him we might become the righteousness of God" (2 Corinthians 5:21). When we were baptized, we turned to Jesus. We were baptized in his name, baptized with him. And when we repent and turn, painful as that may be, we hear the sweet voice of God speaking to us, saying, "This is my son, my daughter, whom I love; I'm pleased with him, with her."

Repentance is hard and painful. But if we walk through that fire, that water of baptism, we come out pure. Loved by God. Right with God. Ready for the kingdom.

"Father, this day move in our hearts to bring us to repentance. May we show by our fruit, our actions, that your kingdom is in us, that we are your children."

MEDITATIONS

TEMPTATION
(MATTHEW 4:1-11)

Day One Reading and Questions:

Then Jesus was led by the Spirit into the desert to be tempted by the devil.

1) *What does it mean to be tempted? From your own experience, describe temptation.*

2) *Since Jesus was the Son of God, could he really be tempted? Is it wrong to be tempted?*

3) *Did the Spirit lead Jesus to temptation? Why? Does God want us to be tempted?*

Day Two Reading and Questions:

²After fasting forty days and forty nights, he was hungry. ³The tempter came to him and said, "If you are the Son of God, tell these stones to become bread."

⁴Jesus answered, "It is written: 'Man does not live on bread alone, but on every word that comes from the mouth of God.'"

1) *Why did Jesus fast? Do you fast? What is the purpose?*

2) Did fasting make Jesus physically weak? Spiritually weak?

3) What's wrong with Jesus turning stones to bread? Where is the sin? Why is this a temptation?

Day Three Reading and Questions:

⁵Then the devil took him to the holy city and had him stand on the highest point of the temple. ⁶"If you are the Son of God," he said, "throw yourself down. For it is written:
 'He will command his angels concerning you,
  and they will lift you up in their hands,
 so that you will not strike your foot against a stone.'"
⁷Jesus answered him, "It is also written: 'Do not put the Lord your God to the test.'"

1) Again, why would throwing himself off the temple be wrong? What is the temptation here?

2) Are you surprised that Satan quotes Scripture? What does this tell us about Bible study?

3) What are some ways we can put God to the test today?

Day Four Reading and Questions:

⁸Again, the devil took him to a very high mountain and showed him all the kingdoms of the world and their splendor. ⁹"All this I will give you," he said, "if you will bow down and worship me."

¹⁰Jesus said to him, "Away from me, Satan! For it is written: 'Worship the Lord your God, and serve him only.' "

¹¹Then the devil left him, and angels came and attended him.

1) Does the devil have all the kingdoms of the world to give? Isn't this God's world?

2) What does it mean to bow down and worship Satan? Is this a one-time act?

3) Angels appeared to Joseph. Now they attend Jesus. Were they there at the temptation or only afterward? What did they do for Jesus?

Day Five Reading and Questions:

Go back and read the entire passage.

1) How are these temptations like ours? How are they different?

2) Pretend you are with Jesus in the desert. How do you picture these temptations? Does Jesus see the devil or hear him differently than how we see and hear him?

3) What is the role of Scripture in fighting temptation?

MEDITATIONS ON MATTHEW 4:1-11.

At first glance, the temptations of Jesus seem to have little similarity to our own. When is the last time you've been tempted to turn rocks to bread, jump off a tall building, or worship Satan?

But a closer look shows that the temptations of Jesus are just like ours. What do we do when we are hungry? In a land of plenty, the answer is obvious. We grab a bite to eat, even if its unhealthy. Thirsty? There's always a water fountain. Are we sexually aroused? The internet is there. What's wrong with meeting our needs? Perhaps nothing. Perhaps everything if it trains us to satisfy all our desires immediately.

But surely God does not want us to be hungry? Yes, he does. That's why Jesus quotes, "He humbled you, causing you to hunger and then feeding you with manna, which neither you nor your fathers had known, to teach you that man does not live by bread alone but on every word that comes from the mouth of the Lord" (Deuteronomy 8:2-3). God caused Israel, he caused Jesus, and he causes us to be hungry. Why? Doesn't he love us?

Of course he does. But what loving father does not at time deny his children? Left to themselves, children will eat too much junk food. We too must learn the lesson Jesus learned in this temptation. We must learn how to be hungry and how to eat. We hunger for all the junk foods of life—money, sex, power, recognition, happiness—instead of hungering for what is truly good and satisfying. God wanted Israel to hunger for him alone. Jesus had learned that lesson. Have we?

What about jumping off the temple? Have you been tempted to jump off a tall building lately? I hope not! So what was the temptation to Jesus? It was to take the easy way out. Jump, angels will protect you, everyone will see you are the Messiah, and you won't have to go to the cross. Satan also tempts us with the easy way out—instant spirituality, automatic holiness, and immediate praise—instead of that long, daily, taking up the cross. We dare not test God by asking for the easy way.

But surely we would not be tempted to bow to Satan, even if he gave us all the kingdoms of the world. Wouldn't we? Don't we bow to him for much less—a moment of pleasure, a little ill-gotten gain, or a brief experience of pride? We need to hear again the words of Scripture and of Jesus. "Worship the Lord your God, and serve him only."

After Jesus overcomes Satan, the angels come and serve him. If we, like Jesus, learn to trust God alone to fill our hungers, to follow God's way, and to serve him only, then we also will have help from above.

"Lord Jesus, since you know temptation, help us when we are tempted. Give us eyes to see the tricks of Satan. Give us hearts to resist. Give us strength to trust."

FOLLOW THE LIGHT
(MATTHEW 4:12-25)

Day One Reading and Questions:

¹²When Jesus heard that John had been put in prison, he returned to Galilee. ¹³Leaving Nazareth, he went and lived in Capernaum, which was by the lake in the area of Zebulun and Naphtali—¹⁴to fulfill what was said through the prophet Isaiah:

¹⁵"Land of Zebulun and land of Naphtali,
   the way to the sea, along the Jordan,
   Galilee of the Gentiles—
¹⁶the people living in darkness
   have seen a great light;
 on those living in the land of the shadow of death
   a light has dawned."

1) John the Baptist has been put in prison for his preaching. What in his preaching would offend the authorities?

2) What comes to mind when you think of light? What are some biblical uses of the word "light"?

3) Darkness here is parallel to the shadow of death. What are the similarities between darkness and death?

Day Two Reading and Questions:

¹⁷From that time on Jesus began to preach, "Repent, for the kingdom of heaven is near."

1) How does the message of Jesus compare to that of John the Baptist?

2) What is the kingdom of heaven?

3) What does Jesus mean when he says the kingdom is near?

Day Three Reading and Questions:

¹⁸As Jesus was walking beside the Sea of Galilee, he saw two brothers, Simon called Peter and his brother Andrew. They were casting a net into the lake, for they were fishermen. ¹⁹"Come, follow me," Jesus said, "and I will make you fishers of men." ²⁰At once they left their nets and followed him.

²¹Going on from there, he saw two other brothers, James son of Zebedee and his brother John. They were in a boat with their father Zebedee, preparing their nets. Jesus called them, ²²and immediately they left the boat and their father and followed him.

1) Why do these men follow Jesus so suddenly?

2) What does it mean to be "fishers of men?"

3) Do you think it was easy for these men to leave their livelihood and their father?

Day Four Reading and Questions:

²³Jesus went throughout Galilee, teaching in their synagogues, preaching the good news of the kingdom, and healing every disease and sickness among the people. ²⁴News about him spread all over Syria, and people brought to him all who were ill with various diseases, those suffering severe pain, the demon-possessed, those having seizures, and the paralyzed, and he healed them. ²⁵Large crowds from Galilee, the Decapolis, Jerusalem, Judea and the region across the Jordan followed him.

1) What three types of work does Jesus do? Should the church today be involved in the same three types?

2) Why did the crowds follow Jesus? Did he want large crowds to follow him?

3) What do you think Jesus taught in the synagogues? What would a typical Jesus lesson look like?

Day Five Reading and Questions:

Go back and read the entire passage.

1) How do the actions of Jesus in this passage display the theme of light?

2) What is the connection among good news, the kingdom, and repentance?

3) How does Jesus fish for people in this section?

MEDITATIONS ON MATTHEW 4:12-25

Light. Jesus came to bring light. For those of us who walk in darkness, who fear the shadow of death, this is indeed good news. But the way of light is the way of repentance. "Turn to God," Jesus says. The reign of God is near. How much do we crave the light? Enough to repent?

Follow. To repent, to turn back to God, is to follow Jesus. And following Jesus, repentance, is always costly. We cannot follow and keep the business, the nets, boat, and fish. We cannot follow and keep the family; we must leave dear old dad in the boat. Ever since this first call, there have been those who call themselves disciples but who will not leave all to follow. We think we can have business, home, and Jesus too. Some even teach that following Jesus will make our business more successful and our homes more stable.

That's not what Jesus said. "Come follow me, and I will make you fishers of men." Another business beacons. The business of love for others. Another family awaits. The family of those who hear the call, who leave, and who follow. Will we obey the call?

Good News! That's what Jesus proclaimed. News of healing, of release from demons, of the kingdom of God. We have turned the gospel into a set of beliefs to affirm or a set of moral laws to follow. We have turned the best of news into the worst of news. No wonder the crowds do not flock to the church as they did to Jesus.

But the good news remains. Light to those in darkness. Healing every disease. God's rule over all. Can you hear the voice of Jesus as he shouts good news today? Turn. Leave. Follow.

"Father, may your kingdom come, your will be done on earth as it is in heaven. This day, turn our lives to you in repentance. May we follow this wonderful good news."

GOD AT WORK
(MATTHEW 5:1-12)

Day One Reading and Questions:

¹Now when he saw the crowds, he went up on a mountainside and sat down. His disciples came to him, ²and he began to teach them saying: ³"Blessed are the poor in spirit,
   for theirs is the kingdom of heaven.
⁴Blessed are those who mourn,
   for they will be comforted."

1) Is Jesus teaching the crowds? Or is he getting away from the crowds to teach a smaller group of disciples?

2) What does it mean to be poor in spirit? Is this different from physical or economic poverty?

3) How can mourning and being blessed go together?

Day Two Reading and Questions:

⁵"Blessed are the meek,
   for they will inherit the earth.
⁶Blessed are those who hunger and thirst for righteousness,
   for they will be filled."

1) Is meekness a virtue or a liability in our society?

2) We expect the meek to be given heaven, but here they inherit the earth. Does this change our view of what "kingdom of heaven" means?

3) What does it mean to hunger and thirst for righteousness?

Day Three Reading and Questions:

[7]"Blessed are the merciful,
  for they will be shown mercy.
[8]Blessed are the pure in heart,
  for they will see God."

1) What is mercy? Think of some specific times when someone showed you mercy.

2) Why do we sometimes find it hard to show mercy? How is mercy different from injustice?

3) What does it mean to be pure in heart?

Day Four Reading and Questions:

[9]"Blessed are the peacemakers,
  for they will be called sons of God.
[10]Blessed are those who are persecuted because of righteousness,
  for theirs is the kingdom of heaven.
[11]Blessed are you when people insult you, persecute you and falsely

say all kinds of evil against you because of me. ¹²Rejoice and be glad, because great is your reward in heaven, for in the same way they persecuted the prophets who were before you."

1) What is the difference among being a peaceful person, being a peaceable person, and being a peacemaker?

2) Think of some specific ways prophets were persecuted. Why would anyone persecute a messenger from God?

3) Why do you think Jesus spent more time explaining, "Blessed are those who are persecuted," than he did on the other beatitudes?

Day Five Reading and Questions:

Go back and read the entire passage.

1) Is it easier to teach a crowd or to make disciples? Which is Jesus most concerned with?

2) What are the Beatitudes? What do they all have in common?

3) Which is more important, the beginning of each beatitude ("blessed are the...") or the end (the reward)?

MEDITATIONS ON MATTHEW 5:1-12

What are the Beatitudes? Are they virtues that the followers of Jesus should strive to possess? Hungering and thirsting for righteousness, being merciful, pure in heart, and peacemakers—all sound like qualities we should cultivate to follow Jesus.

Or are the Beatitudes circumstances over which we have no control? Surely, we should not cultivate mourning or persecution. Grief comes uninvited. Persecution of the righteous comes (by definition) when we do not deserve it.

Then there are the Beatitudes that can go either way. Does "poor in spirit" refer to an attitude we can develop or to circumstances like material poverty that we cannot fully control? Are the meek that way because the world has oppressed them? Or is meekness a quality we should strive for?

There are no easy answers here. That may be the point of Jesus' cryptic words. Jesus is not giving attitudes to make us happy. Neither is he recommending complete passivity in the face of injustice. Instead, what all the Beatitudes have in common is they call us to be open to the work of God. Even if the world grinds us down with poverty, meekness, grief, and persecution, we trust that God will act. The kingdom of heaven is ours, the reign of God where he brings us comfort, gives us the earth, fills us with righteousness, shows us mercy, reveals his face, and calls us his children. The Beatitudes do not call us to greater effort to achieve righteousness (that's the approach of the scribes and Pharisees), but they demand that we surrender our will to the will of God. In the words of Therese of Lisieux, "Jesus does not demand great deeds, but only gratitude and self-surrender."

In the Beatitudes, Jesus opens up for us a brand new world, a world he calls the kingdom of God. He calls us as his disciples to follow him into that kingdom. He asks us not to abandon our world or hide from its sorrows, but to embrace the world with all its griefs, knowing that God is at work transforming that world. The world of mourning, persecution, hunger, and poverty is becoming the kingdom of our Lord and of his Christ.

"Father, give us trust in your work in our world and in ourselves. May we daily give ourselves to you, not in heroic virtue, but in humble self-surrender."

HIGHER RIGHTEOUSNESS
(MATTHEW 5:13-20)

Day One Reading and Questions:

¹³"You are the salt of the earth. But if the salt loses its saltiness, how can it be made salty again? It is no longer good for anything, except to be thrown out and trampled by men."

1) List as many uses you can for salt.

2) What does the phrase "salt of the earth" mean to most people? Is that what it means here?

3) What does it mean for us as salt to lose our saltiness? What would that loss look like?

Day Two Reading and Questions:

¹⁴"You are the light of the world. A city on a hill cannot be hidden. ¹⁵Neither do people light a lamp and put it under a bowl. Instead they put it on its stand, and it gives light to everyone in the house. ¹⁶In the same way, let your light shine before men, that they may see your good deeds and praise your Father in heaven."

1) What do light and a city on a hill have in common? What is the point Jesus is making?

2) Think of some ways we can hide our lights as Christians.

3) What is the danger in letting others see our good deeds? Why should we let them see?

Day Three Reading and Questions:

[17]"Do not think that I have come to abolish the Law or the Prophets; I have not come to abolish them but to fulfill them. [18]I tell you the truth, until heaven and earth disappear, not the smallest letter, not the least stroke of a pen, will by any means disappear from the Law until everything is accomplished."

1) Do we sometimes think Jesus came to abolish the Old Testament laws (the Law and the Prophets)? Why do we think so?

2) According to Jesus, what is the value of the Old Testament for his followers?

3) What does it mean to fulfill or accomplish the Law?

Day Four Reading and Questions:

[19]"Anyone who breaks one of the least of these commandments and teaches others to do the same will be called least in the kingdom of heaven, but whoever practices and teaches these commands will be called great in the kingdom of heaven. [20]For I tell you that unless your

righteousness surpasses that of the Pharisees and the teachers of the law, you will certainly not enter the kingdom of heaven."

1) *Why would anyone teach others to break commands? Can you think of situations where you have heard advice from a Christian to break a command?*

2) *Do we think of the Pharisees as righteous? Did those in Jesus day think the Pharisees were righteous? Why do we have differing views?*

3) *Describe a righteousness that is greater than that of the Pharisees and teachers of the Law.*

Day Five Reading and Questions:

Go back and read the entire passage.

1) *What exactly is Jesus demanding in this passage? Perfection? That we try harder to keep the commands?*

2) *How does this "higher righteousness" relate to being salt and light?*

3) *How is the Law fulfilled or accomplished in us?*

MEDITATIONS ON MATTHEW 5:13-20

Isn't this an impossible standard? Our righteousness must surpass that of the Pharisees. We cannot break even the smallest of commands. Is Jesus demanding perfection? Does he want a level of obedience we cannot achieve, no matter how we try?

If so, then the only response to the words of Jesus is guilt. We do not measure up. But what if Jesus means something else? What if what he demands is not some impossible standard, but a living, daily relationship?

How can our righteousness exceed that of the Pharisees and teachers of the Law? What did their "righteousness" consist of? The rest of Matthew makes clear that they thought themselves righteous because they externally kept the commands of God, but their hearts were not right with him. Jesus points us back to the reason for commands. They all have to do with genuine relationship with God and with others.

That's where salt and light come in. We are salt and light not through our own power and effort. We do not act like salt; we are salt. We do not act like light; we are light, and so we shine. Our righteousness comes from within as a gift from God. He makes us salt and light. We embrace what he has made us, keeping our saltiness and letting our light shine. We keep commands because God lives in us. We do good deeds so others will see and praise God, not praise us.

Too many times our response to the commands of God is the same as the Pharisees. We think we must simply try harder to obey. But Jesus in us fulfils the commands, the Law and Prophets. So in the words of Augustine in his *Confessions*, we pray, "Grant what you command, and command what you will." The higher righteousness comes from a heart turned to God.

"Father, turn my heart toward you. This day, may I live out the righteousness of Jesus in me, tasting like his salt, shining with his light."

INSIDE-OUT OBEDIENCE
(MATTHEW 5:21-37)

Day One Reading and Questions:

[21]"You have heard that it was said to the people long ago, 'Do not murder, and anyone who murders will be subject to judgment.' [22]But I tell you that anyone who is angry with his brother will be subject to judgment. Again, anyone who says to his brother, 'Raca,' is answerable to the Sanhedrin. But anyone who says, 'You fool!' will be in danger of the fire of hell.

[23]"Therefore, if you are offering your gift at the altar and there remember that your brother has something against you, [24]leave your gift there in front of the altar. First go and be reconciled to your brother; then come and offer your gift.

[25]"Settle matters quickly with your adversary who is taking you to court. Do it while you are still with him on the way, or he may hand you over to the judge, and the judge may hand you over to the officer, and you may be thrown into prison. [26]I tell you the truth, you will not get out until you have paid the last penny."

1) What is the relationship between what we say to people and murder? Is this a mere prohibition of saying "Raca" or "fool"? What is really condemned here?

2) How does relationship with others affect worship? What makes worship acceptable to God?

3) Who is the judge who will cast us into prison if we do not reconcile with our adversary? What does this imply about forgiveness?

Day Two Reading and Questions:

[27]"You have heard that it was said, 'Do not commit adultery.' [28]But I tell you that anyone who looks at a woman lustfully has already committed adultery with her in his heart. [29]If your right eye causes you to sin, gouge it out and throw it away. It is better for you to lose one part of your body than for your whole body to be thrown into hell. [30]And if your right hand causes you to sin, cut it off and throw it away. It is better for you to lose one part of your body than for your whole body to go into hell."

1) What is lust? Is it the same as sexual attraction?

2) How is this passage similar to the one on murder?

3) Are we literally supposed to cut off body parts to avoid sin? If not, what is Jesus saying?

Day Three Reading and Questions:

[31]"It has been said, 'Anyone who divorces his wife must give her a certificate of divorce.' [32]But I tell you that anyone who divorces his wife, except for marital unfaithfulness, causes her to become an adulteress, and anyone who marries the divorced woman commits adultery."

1) Is this passage hard to understand? If not, why have we made it so hard?

2) Does this make divorce the unpardonable sin? What would it mean to repent of divorce?

3) How is this passage like the one on murder and the one on adultery? What is Jesus commanding here?

Day Four Reading and Questions:

³³"Again, you have heard that it was said to the people long ago, 'Do not break your oath, but keep the oaths you have made to the Lord.' ³⁴But I tell you, Do not swear at all: either by heaven, for it is God's throne; ³⁵or by the earth, for it is his footstool; or by Jerusalem, for it is the city of the Great King. ³⁶And do not swear by your head, for you cannot make even one hair white or black. ³⁷Simply let your 'Yes' be 'Yes,' and your 'No,' 'No'; anything beyond this comes from the evil one."

1) What is swearing? Why would someone feel a need to take an oath?

2) What is the point of not swearing by heaven, Jerusalem, or our heads?

3) What does it mean to let our "Yes" be "yes" and our "No," "No"? Put this command in your own words.

Day Five Reading and Questions:

Go back and read the entire passage.

1) Is Jesus trying to make the Law harder?

2) When Jesus says, "You have heard it said..." where had they heard it? Who said it? Is Jesus trying to question the Law of God or question the interpretations of the Pharisees and others?

3) What does Jesus say in this section about the heart?

MEDITATIONS ON MATTHEW 5:21-37

Do not murder. Do not commit adultery. Do not divorce. Do not swear.

Isn't that what Christianity's all about? We must be good people (or at least, we must not be bad people). We must avoid sin (or at least the big sins).

But aren't most of us pretty good? We know few murderers. We are not really tempted to kill anyone. Adultery? That may give more of us trouble, but most of us are faithful husbands and wives. Divorce? Well, that's different, isn't it. Many of us are divorced. Sometimes things just don't work out. Taking oaths? Most of us never swear by anything.

So how are we doing with this list? Murder. Adultery. Divorce. Swearing. Do we avoid two out of four? Do we score 100%, refusing to commit any of these sins? What is the acceptable score to Jesus? Will he not forgive us?

But Jesus sets the standard higher. It's not enough not to murder. We must not even be angry. Lust is as bad as adultery. Don't divorce at all, except for unfaithfulness. Do not take any oaths. Who can meet these standards? Who can be this good?

No one. At least, we cannot on our own power. So is that what Jesus is doing, setting impossible standards? No. He is saying something more profound, that relationship with God is not about being good enough. What's more, he's saying something about where true obedience and genuine righteousness begins.

It springs from the heart. Murder is not random and spontaneous. It begins with nursing anger in our hearts. Adultery does not just happen. It grows out of uncontrolled desires deep within us. Divorce is never sudden. It stems from years of resentment and selfishness. Dishonesty does not spring from breaking oaths, but from a divided heart that cannot say "yes" or "no" and mean it unequivocally.

God has never wanted external obedience. He wants our hearts. Relationship with God has never been about "do's and don'ts." It has always been about love and forgiveness. What makes us right with God is not keeping commands as best we can, asking for forgiveness when we fail, and then living most of our lives the way we please. God wants all of us, from the inside out.

"Father, do forgive, for we are sinful. Forgive our attempts to please you with outward obedience. Change our hearts, O God, to love as you are love."

PERFECT LOVE
(MATTHEW 5:38-48)

Day One Reading and Questions:

³⁸"You have heard that it was said, 'Eye for eye, and tooth for tooth.' ³⁹But I tell you, Do not resist an evil person. If someone strikes you on the right cheek, turn to him the other also."

1) What is the point of "Eye for eye, and tooth for tooth?" Does this promote or limit vengeance?

2) Is it true that we should not resist an evil person? Can we call the police? What about national security?

3) Is a backhand implied by being struck on the right cheek? If so, what does that mean? Can we strike back if hit on the left cheek?

Day Two Reading and Questions:

⁴⁰"And if someone wants to sue you and take your tunic, let him have your cloak as well. ⁴¹If someone forces you to go one mile, go with him two miles. ⁴²Give to the one who asks you, and do not turn away from the one who wants to borrow from you."

1) Does this mean that Christians should never fight a lawsuit? Must

we let other people cheat us? Should we not demand our rights?

2) *What does it mean to go the second mile? Give examples.*

3) *Do you give to everyone and every organization that asks you for money? Is this possible? What if people are conning you?*

Day Three Reading and Questions:

⁴³"You have heard that it was said, 'Love your neighbor and hate your enemy.' ⁴⁴But I tell you: Love your enemies and pray for those who persecute you, ⁴⁵that you may be sons of your Father in heaven. He causes his sun to rise on the evil and the good, and sends rain on the righteous and the unrighteous."

1) *Can we really love our enemies? Does this mean we have warm affection for them? What does it mean?*

2) *What should we pray concerning our persecutors? Write a brief prayer for someone who has hurt you.*

3) *What is the point of God sending sun and rain on everyone? How do we act like God here?*

Day Four Reading and Questions:

⁴⁶"If you love those who love you, what reward will you get? Are not even the tax collectors doing that? ⁴⁷And if you greet only your brothers, what are you doing more than others? Do not even pagans do that? ⁴⁸Be perfect, therefore, as your heavenly Father is perfect."

1) *It is human nature to love those who love us. Jesus calls us to something greater. What does this say about our view of what it means to be human?*

2) *What comes to mind when you hear the word, "perfect"? Isn't it true that no one is perfect?*

3) *Is Jesus demanding perfection from us in everything? Or is this a particular area where we must be perfect?*

Day Five Reading and Questions:

Go back and read the entire passage.

1) *Do we try to soften or explain away the statements of Jesus in this passage? Why?*

2) *What is your reaction to what Jesus says here? Guilt? Rejection? Confusion?*

3) *Is there any way we can do what Jesus demands?*

MEDITATIONS ON MATTHEW 5:38-48

Of all the demanding statements of Jesus, these may be the most offensive. They sound so radical that we reject them as ridiculous. "Turn the other cheek." "Do not resist an evil person." "Give to anyone who asks you." "Love your enemies." "Be perfect as your heavenly Father is perfect."

So we try to explain away those statements. Surely there are times when we must resist evil. Isn't that why we have police? What about Hitler or Stalin or the madman of the moment—shouldn't we resist them? Obviously we should not give to everyone who asks for help. Some of them are con men and liars. Sure, we should love our enemies, but we must defend ourselves, our country, and our way of life. We don't have ill feelings toward those we bomb. And we all know that nobody is perfect.

But what if, instead of explaining Jesus away, we were to take him seriously? What if God's love, the love that sends sunshine and rain to righteous and unrighteous, what if that love were perfected in us? What if God so worked in our hearts that we could meet violence with good will? What if God in us treated compassionately those who asked us for help? What would we do? How would we live?

The higher righteousness that comes from the inside out gives us supernatural strength to love. Strength to overcome evil with good. Strength to give when others simply take. Strength to be hurt, cheated, and unjustly punished. Elsewhere, Jesus calls it taking up the cross.

"Father, this day may I die to self. Give me that suffering love of Jesus. Give me your perfect love."

MEDITATIONS

SECRET RIGHTEOUSNESS
(MATTHEW 6:1-18)

Day One Reading and Questions:

¹"Be careful not to do your 'acts of righteousness' before men, to be seen by them. If you do, you will have no reward from your Father in heaven.

²"So when you give to the needy, do not announce it with trumpets, as the hypocrites do in the synagogues and on the streets, to be honored by men. I tell you the truth, they have received their reward in full. ³But when you give to the needy, do not let your left hand know what your right hand is doing, ⁴so that your giving may be in secret. Then your Father, who sees what is done in secret, will reward you."

1) Does the command to not let our acts of righteousness be seen by others contradict the command to let others see our good works (Matthew 5:16)? Why not?

2) Can we literally not let our left hand know what our right is doing? If not, what does Jesus mean by this command?

3) What two types of reward are mentioned here? Can we have both? Why or why not?

Day Two Reading and Questions:

⁵"And when you pray, do not be like the hypocrites, for they love to pray standing in the synagogues and on the street corners to be seen by men. I tell you the truth, they have received their reward in full. ⁶But when you pray, go into your room, close the door and pray to your Father, who is unseen. Then your Father, who sees what is done in secret, will reward you. ⁷And when you pray, do not keep on babbling like pagans, for they think they will be heard because of their many words. ⁸Do not be like them, for your Father knows what you need before you ask him."

1) Should we ever pray in front of others? How about leading a group in prayer? Is it wrong? Can it be?

2) What is the point of saying that God is unseen? What does this say about prayer?

3) Is Jesus condemning long prayers? Did he not sometimes pray all night? What is the difference between an extended time of prayer and praying with many words?

Day Three Reading and Questions:

⁹"This, then, is how you should pray:
  'Our Father in heaven,
  hallowed be your name,
  ¹⁰your kingdom come,
  your will be done
  on earth as it is in heaven.

MEDITATIONS

[11]Give us today our daily bread.
[12]Forgive us our debts,
    as we also have forgiven our debtors.
[13]And lead us not into temptation,
    but deliver us from the evil one.' "

[14]For if you forgive men when they sin against you, your heavenly Father will also forgive you. [15]But if you do not forgive men their sins, your Father will not forgive your sins.

1) We pray for God's kingdom to come. What does that mean? What will it look like when the kingdom comes?

2) Does God tempt us? Does he keep us from temptation? Didn't the Spirit lead Jesus into the desert to be tempted (see Matthew 4:1)? Why should we pray not to be led into temptation if temptation makes us stronger?

3) Why does Jesus comment on forgiveness and not on the other parts of this prayer?

Day Four Reading and Questions:

[16]"When you fast, do not look somber as the hypocrites do, for they disfigure their faces to show men they are fasting. I tell you the truth, they have received their reward in full. [17]But when you fast, put oil on your head and wash your face, [18]so that it will not be obvious to men that you are fasting, but only to your Father, who is unseen; and your Father, who sees what is done in secret, will reward you."

1) Does Jesus expect his followers to fast?

2) What are the purposes of fasting?

3) Why do so few contemporary Christians fast? Do you fast? Why or why not?

Day Five Reading and Questions:

Go back and read the entire passage.

1) What does Jesus mean by doing our righteous acts in secret? Should we be ashamed of these acts? Should we never go public with them?

2) Why do churches and Christian organizations name windows, buildings, and funds after big donors? Is this not violating what Jesus says?

3) What is it that makes us want to be recognized for our goodness?

MEDITATIONS ON MATTHEW 6:1-18

Secret righteousness. That's what Jesus commands. Not "secret" in the sense of absolutely hidden (we are to let our light shine), and not secret in the contemporary sense of "private." Jesus is not recommending that we keep religion in its place—privately in the home or at church, not at work, school, and the voting booth.

Instead, by "secret" Jesus means we should avoid that pleasurable sensation of being recognized for our righteousness. Yet almost every church, Christian college, and parachurch ministry have windows, funds, and buildings named after big donors. We might look down on those who give to be "immortalized" on a plaque or cornerstone, but we always take their money. Are we any better? Don't we all have a secret desire to be recognized for our good works? Have you ever gone out of your way to help someone and told absolutely no one about it? Did you find that silence hard?

What does it take to achieve the higher righteousness that Jesus demands? Certainly, it takes giving, praying, and fasting. Fasting? Yes, just an ordinary path to righteousness in Jesus' day. Today we consider those who fast extraordinary in their righteousness.

But even these actions that are intended to open our hearts to God can be corrupted by the depth of our selfishness. Spiritual disciplines can become badges of honor. We can do them to be seen by others.

The solution is not to stop giving, praying, and fasting. Many of us need to begin these practices, not end them. The solution is to remember that these are ways we open ourselves to the God who makes us righteous when we do not deserve it.

"God of love, forgive our pride in being 'good.' Lead us to yourself, the only source of true goodness."

TREASURE
(MATTHEW 6:19-34)

Day One Reading and Questions:

¹⁹"Do not store up for yourselves treasures on earth, where moth and rust destroy, and where thieves break in and steal. ²⁰But store up for yourselves treasures in heaven, where moth and rust do not destroy, and where thieves do not break in and steal. ²¹For where your treasure is, there your heart will be also."

1) What are the ways that earthly treasure is taken from us? In light of this, why do we invest our money?

2) What does it mean that our hearts are where our treasure is? What does "heart" mean here?

3) How do we lay up treasure in heaven? How does this relate to the rest of the Sermon on the Mount?

Day Two Reading and Questions:

²²"The eye is the lamp of the body. If your eyes are good, your whole body will be full of light. ²³But if your eyes are bad, your whole body will be full of darkness. If then the light within you is darkness, how great is that darkness!

MEDITATIONS

[24]"No one can serve two masters. Either he will hate the one and love the other, or he will be devoted to the one and despise the other. You cannot serve both God and Money."

1) *What do our eyes have to do with treasure and money? What is the difference here between good eyes and bad eyes?*

2) *What does it mean to serve Money? Name someone you think serves Money.*

3) *We know we cannot serve God and Money, but can we have God and money? If so, how is it possible? How can you have money and not serve it?*

Day Three Reading and Questions:

[25]"Therefore I tell you, do not worry about your life, what you will eat or drink; or about your body, what you will wear. Is not life more important than food, and the body more important than clothes? [26]Look at the birds of the air; they do not sow or reap or store away in barns, and yet your heavenly Father feeds them. Are you not much more valuable than they? [27]Who of you by worrying can add a single hour to his life?

[28]"And why do you worry about clothes? See how the lilies of the field grow. They do not labor or spin. [29]Yet I tell you that not even Solomon in all his splendor was dressed like one of these. [30]If that is how God clothes the grass of the field, which is here today and tomorrow is thrown into the fire, will he not much more clothe you, O you of little faith? [31]So do not worry, saying, 'What shall we eat?' or 'What shall we drink?' or 'What shall we wear?' [32]For the pagans run after all these things, and your heavenly Father knows that you need them."

1) Why do we spend so much time and effort worrying about food and clothing? What does this say about our faith?

2) God feeds the birds. Does this mean birds do no work at all? Do we have to work for God to feed us? Does this mean we feed ourselves?

3) Does worry ever help a situation?

Day Four Reading and Questions:

³³"But seek first his kingdom and his righteousness, and all these things will be given to you as well. ³⁴Therefore do not worry about tomorrow, for tomorrow will worry about itself. Each day has enough trouble of its own."

1) What does it mean to seek God's kingdom first? If we seek it first, can we then seek these other things?

2) Are we not to plan for tomorrow? When does planning become worry?

3) "Each day has enough trouble of its own." Is this an encouraging statement?

Day Five Reading and Questions:

Go back and read the entire passage.

1) Why do we care about money? Would we be foolish not to care?

2) What is the relationship between seeking the kingdom first and not

worrying about tomorrow?

3) *Where do you live? In the past? In the future? One day at a time?*

MEDITATIONS ON MATTHEW 6:19-34

"You cannot serve both God and Money."
Another tough statement from Jesus that we explain away. Of course, we know greedy people. They're the ones who make more than we do. We don't serve money.

But we worry about it. We spend most of our life making it. We spend it. We spend money we don't have with mortgages and credit cards. We look to see how the stock market is doing. We wonder if we can make it to the end of the month. How will we send the kids to college? Will we be able to retire? Why is there never enough?

Why do we care about money? We would be fools not to. But Jesus says we are foolish if we do worry about money. Money promises pleasure, security, success, and happiness. It delivers on none of its promises. Pleasures do not last. Thieves break in. Moth and rust destroy.

We give our attention, our time, and our hearts to money. Instead we should put our trust in heaven, in the kingdom, in righteousness, in God alone. He gives pleasures that can never be taken from us. He provides absolute security. He grants the gifts of success and happiness.

"Do not care about money." Foolish advice? Unrealistic? How can one actually live that way? Only one day at a time. Do we have enough to live on today? Isn't today, right now, when we live? Our worries about money are part of a larger problem. We live too much the future, anticipating its troubles, instead of living today in the kingdom. Trust God today.

"Loving Father, you have provided what I need thus far in life. May I trust you to provide this day."

DO UNTO OTHERS
(MATTHEW 7:1-12)

Day One Reading and Questions:

¹"Do not judge, or you too will be judged. ²For in the same way you judge others, you will be judged, and with the measure you use, it will be measured to you.

³"Why do you look at the speck of sawdust in your brother's eye and pay no attention to the plank in your own eye? ⁴How can you say to your brother, 'Let me take the speck out of your eye,' when all the time there is a plank in your own eye? ⁵You hypocrite, first take the plank out of your own eye, and then you will see clearly to remove the speck from your brother's eye."

1) *Should we never judge the actions of others? What kind of judgment is Jesus condemning?*

2) *Is it a kind thing to take a speck of sawdust out of another's eye? Is Jesus suggesting we ignore faults in others?*

3) *Do we naturally tend to hold others to the same standard as ourselves? To a lower standard? To a higher one? Why?*

Day Two Reading and Questions:

[6]"Do not give dogs what is sacred; do not throw your pearls to pigs. If you do, they may trample them under their feet, and then turn and tear you to pieces."

1) What comes to mind when you think of dogs and pigs? Are these terms complimentary?

2) Why would Jesus call people dogs or pigs? Isn't that judgmental?

3) Have you ever done something good for someone only to have them turn on you? How did that make you feel?

Day Three Reading and Questions:

[7]"Ask and it will be given to you; seek and you will find; knock and the door will be opened to you. [8]For everyone who asks receives; he who seeks finds; and to him who knocks, the door will be opened.
[9]"Which of you, if his son asks for bread, will give him a stone? [10]Or if he asks for a fish, will give him a snake? [11]If you, then, though you are evil, know how to give good gifts to your children, how much more will your Father in heaven give good gifts to those who ask him!"

1) Do we get everything we ask God for? Why not?

2) Jesus says we are evil. What does this say about original sin? Predestination? Choice?

3) What is the point of saying we are evil? What is the contrast?

Day Four Reading and Questions:

¹²"So in everything, do to others what you would have them do to you, for this sums up the Law and the Prophets."

1) What keeps us from consistently following the golden rule?

2) How does this verse relate to what has gone before it about judging?

3) If this rule sums up the Law and the Prophets, then why did Israel and why do we need all those other biblical laws?

Day Five Reading and Questions:

Go back and read the entire passage.

1) Do you find it hard to avoid judging others? What would help us judge as we want to be judged?

2) When others harm us, do we usually think they did it on purpose? When we harm others, is it usually accidental or purposeful?

3) How does, "Ask, Seek, Knock" relate to the golden rule?

MEDITATIONS ON MATTHEW 7:1-12

"Do to others what you would have them do to you."
We call it the golden rule. Jesus says it sums up the Law and the Prophets. In other words, all of Scripture is contained in these few words.

"Do to others what you would have them do to you." It sounds good, but exactly what does it look like?

It looks like refusing to judge others by standards harsher than we use to judge ourselves. If you're walking down the hall at school or at the office and you bump into someone, you immediately apologize, feeling sure that they will know that it was unintentional. But if they bump into you, spilling your coffee on your clothes, you may immediately assume they did it on purpose, even if they apologize. We may do this even more quickly with words. If we snap at someone, we want them to forget it, knowing that we are just having a bad day. If they snap at us, we hold on to that grievance for days on end.

Why? Why do we want others to dismiss our actions as accidental when we assume they do everything on purpose? Because we do not judge them the way we wish to be judged. We do not do to others what we wish for them to do to us. It is human nature, fallen and sinful human nature, to be able to see more clearly faults in others than we see them in ourselves. We must sometimes look hard to see logs in our eyes.

This does not mean we never point out specks in the eyes of our brothers and sisters. Pointing out specks can be an act of love. Specks in the eye hurt. They can make us blind. But we point them out gently, with mercy, because we want others to do the same for us.

But what about dogs and pigs? How do they relate to "doing unto others"? If we truly treat others the way we want to be treated, it sometimes calls for tough love. At times we need to be confronted about the logs in our eyes. We also need to be aware when others have logs, or worse, they have bad hearts. We should judge as God does, with mercy, but we are not called naively to ignore evil. There are pigs and dogs who will not accept what is holy.

Doing unto others what we would have them do to us is difficult, so difficult that it drives us to rely on God's power. He is a Father who gives good gifts. If we ask, seek, and knock, he will even fill us with his mercy, mercy enough to do to others what we want done to us. The Father of mercy makes us merciful.

"Father, you know how easy it is for us to see through selfish eyes, full of logs. We ask, seek, and knock to receive your love so we might show it to others."

MEDITATIONS

DOING THE WORD
(MATTHEW 7:13-29)

Day One Reading and Questions:

[13]"Enter through the narrow gate. For wide is the gate and broad is the road that leads to destruction, and many enter through it. [14]But small is the gate and narrow the road that leads to life, and only a few find it."

1) *Why would anyone willingly follow the path to destruction? Why do many follow it?*

2) *What makes the way to life narrow? The difficulties of the teachings of Jesus? A narrowness in the mercy of God? High Standards? Or is it something else?*

3) *What does the invitation to enter the narrow gate imply? Are all invited to enter? How?*

Day Two Reading and Questions:

[15]"Watch out for false prophets. They come to you in sheep's clothing, but inwardly they are ferocious wolves. [16]By their fruit you will recognize them. Do people pick grapes from thornbushes, or figs from thistles? [17]Likewise every good tree bears good fruit, but a bad

tree bears bad fruit. ¹⁸A good tree cannot bear bad fruit, and a bad tree cannot bear good fruit. ¹⁹Every tree that does not bear good fruit is cut down and thrown into the fire. ²⁰Thus, by their fruit you will recognize them."

> 1) What comes to mind when you hear, "false teachers?" Have you known those falsely accused of being false teachers? What makes one a genuine false teacher?
>
> 2) What is the fruit by which we recognize false teachers? Does this involve more than whether they are right or wrong on a point of doctrine? How long does it take to tell good fruit from bad? Is this a snap judgment?
>
> 3) How is judging fruit different from the evil judging Jesus earlier condemns?

Day Three Reading and Questions:

²¹"Not everyone who says to me, 'Lord, Lord,' will enter the kingdom of heaven, but only he who does the will of my Father who is in heaven. ²²Many will say to me on that day, 'Lord, Lord, did we not prophesy in your name, and in your name drive out demons and perform many miracles?' ²³Then I will tell them plainly, 'I never knew you. Away from me, you evildoers!' "

> 1) How could someone convince themselves they are right with Jesus when they are not? Is self-deception a danger for all of us? How can we avoid it?
>
> 2) Jesus is talking about doing what he says, but these people have done many things for Jesus, even miracles. Do good works bring us

into the kingdom? Why or why not?

3) *What does Jesus mean when he says he does not know them? What does it take to be known by Jesus?*

Day Four Reading and Questions:

²⁴"Therefore everyone who hears these words of mine and puts them into practice is like a wise man who built his house on the rock. ²⁵The rain came down, the streams rose, and the winds blew and beat against that house; yet it did not fall, because it had its foundation on the rock. ²⁶But everyone who hears these words of mine and does not put them into practice is like a foolish man who built his house on sand. ²⁷The rain came down, the streams rose, and the winds blew and beat against that house, and it fell with a great crash."

²⁸When Jesus had finished saying these things, the crowds were amazed at his teaching, ²⁹because he taught as one who had authority, and not as their teachers of the law.

1) *What makes the wise man wise and the foolish man foolish in this passage? How does that relate to doing what Jesus says?*

2) *What gives Jesus his authority to teach? What makes his words sound authoritative? How do his words differ from other religious teachers?*

3) *What is the connection between faith or trust and obedience?*

Day Five Reading and Questions:

Go back and read the entire passage.

1) Name several things from this passage that keep us from entering the narrow way.

2) What do you find most difficult in following Jesus? What can help you with that difficulty?

3) What does it mean to recognize the authority of Jesus? What must we do to truly follow his authority?

MEDITATIONS ON MATTHEW 7:13-29

Will we do what we know we ought to do? Will we follow the path of righteousness? Will we practice the words of Jesus?

These are real questions. It's not that we do not know the path of Jesus. We have heard his teachings. It's not that this path of obedience is beyond us. It is the path of grace. God lavishes on us the gift of obedience, empowering us with the higher righteousness. Jesus walks beside us on the path with every step. The Holy Spirit works in us to make us holy.

So why is following this path so hard? Why do many follow the path to destruction? Why do so few follow the path to life?

Part of our difficulty in following the path to life lies with those who would deceive us. There are false teachers out there. They are not sincerely mistaken about fine points of doctrine. They are intentionally out to deceive us to gain power, recognition, and money for themselves. If we are not careful, they will devour us like wolves. This is not a call to paranoia or suspicion of everyone we meet. It is a warning to inspect fruit, to test Christian teachers by their long-term behavior and actions.

More frightening than false teachers is the possibility of self-deception. On the day the kingdom comes, some will expect to enter it because of the amazing things they have done for Jesus. But Jesus does not know them. He even calls them "evildoers."

Are we deceiving ourselves? It's a frightening question, because if we are really good at self-deception, how would we know?

So are we to live in constant fear that we might miss the kingdom? No. we are to live in trust. Trust that Jesus does know us. But trust must be lived. We must not deceive ourselves into thinking we know Jesus just because we have heard his words. We must be wise and practice them. If we truly think he speaks with authority, then we must let him have authority over all that we are.

"Lord Jesus, rule my life today. Place your holy words in my heart and life. Give me the power to hear and to do."

ASTONISHED

(MATTHEW 8:1-17)

Day One Reading and Questions:

¹When he came down from the mountainside, large crowds followed him. ²A man with leprosy came and knelt before him and said, "Lord, if you are willing, you can make me clean."

³Jesus reached out his hand and touched the man. "I am willing," he said. "Be clean!" Immediately he was cured of his leprosy. ⁴Then Jesus said to him, "See that you don't tell anyone. But go, show yourself to the priest and offer the gift Moses commanded, as a testimony to them."

1) What do you know about leprosy? How did those in Jesus' day treat lepers?

2) Why does the leper ask Jesus to make him clean instead of asking to be healed?

3) Why does Jesus tell the leper not to tell anyone but the priest of this cure?

Day Two Reading and Questions:

⁵When Jesus had entered Capernaum, a centurion came to him, asking for help. ⁶"Lord," he said, "my servant lies at home paralyzed and in terrible suffering."

⁷Jesus said to him, "I will go and heal him."

⁸The centurion replied, "Lord, I do not deserve to have you come under my roof. But just say the word, and my servant will be healed. ⁹For I myself am a man under authority, with soldiers under me. I tell this one, 'Go,' and he goes; and that one, 'Come,' and he comes. I say to my servant, 'Do this,' and he does it."

1) What was the job of a centurion in Israel? What religion did the centurion have?

2) What did the centurion understand about the authority of Jesus? What personal experiences let him understand this?

3) How does this recognition of authority compare with that of Matthew 7:29?

Day Three Reading and Questions:

¹⁰When Jesus heard this, he was astonished and said to those following him, "I tell you the truth, I have not found anyone in Israel with such great faith. ¹¹I say to you that many will come from the east and the west, and will take their places at the feast with Abraham, Isaac and Jacob in the kingdom of heaven. ¹²But the subjects of the kingdom will be thrown outside, into the darkness, where there will be weeping and gnashing of teeth."

¹³Then Jesus said to the centurion, "Go! It will be done just as you believed it would." And his servant was healed at that very hour.

1) Why is Jesus astonished at the centurion? What does it say about Jesus, that he could be so astonished?

2) What is the point of many coming from east and west to the great banquet?

3) What separates those at the feast from those thrown out?

Day Four Reading and Questions:

¹⁴When Jesus came into Peter's house, he saw Peter's mother-in-law lying in bed with a fever. ¹⁵He touched her hand and the fever left her, and she got up and began to wait on him.

¹⁶When evening came, many who were demon-possessed were brought to him, and he drove out the spirits with a word and healed all the sick. ¹⁷This was to fulfill what was spoken through the prophet Isaiah:
"He took up our infirmities
    and carried our diseases."

1) How did Jesus heal Peter's mother-in-law? Is that significant?

2) Jesus drives out demons with a word. Does this relate to his authority? How?

3) The quote from Isaiah says Jesus carried our diseases. Does he heal all our diseases? What does that passage mean?

Day Five Reading and Questions:

Go back and read the entire passage.

1) Are you ever astonished at how good or how faithful people are? Give examples. If not, what does this say about our hearts?

2) Why is the centurion such an unlikely person to have such faith? Do we sometimes stereotype people in ways that keep us from seeing them? Give examples.

3) *What does this entire section teach us about the authority of Jesus? Does Jesus still have that authority? How does he show it in your life?*

MEDITATIONS ON MATTHEW 8:1-17

"He was astonished."

Jesus could be surprised. He didn't live a pre-programmed life. He was not so bored that he did not pay attention. He lived life with eyes wide open to the possibilities of the day.

He could even be pleasantly surprised at people. Can we? Or have we become so cynical that we think no one can really change? Our family and friends are so familiar that we can even finish their sentences for them. They tell the same old stories, make the same old mistakes, and live the same old lives.

Perhaps even strangers can no longer surprise us. We think we have human nature figured out. But Jesus is astonished by a stranger, a centurion, one who is a stranger to the people of God. A soldier of Rome, sent to oppress Israel. A Gentile, outside the fold of God.

But this Gentile, from a pagan, idol-worshipping background, has more faith than anyone in Israel. And some in Israel have great faith. The leper believes Jesus can make him clean. Peter believes enough to leave his nets and follow Jesus. Jesus heals his mother-in-law. Many who are sick and demon-possessed have the faith to come to Jesus for healing.

But this centurion outdoes them all. He asks healing not for himself but for his servant. He humbly does not want to trouble Jesus to come to his house to heal him. "Just say the word, and my servant will be healed." He sees a depth of power in Jesus that others do not see.

Are we ever surprised by the great faith of others? Are we inspired by their overwhelming trust to be more faithful ourselves?

"Lord Jesus, increase our faith. May we trust you to do more than we can ask or imagine this day."

FOLLOWING JESUS
(MATTHEW 8:18-9:12)

Day One Reading and Questions:

[18]When Jesus saw the crowd around him, he gave orders to cross to the other side of the lake. [19]Then a teacher of the law came to him and said, "Teacher, I will follow you wherever you go."

[20]Jesus replied, "Foxes have holes and birds of the air have nests, but the Son of Man has no place to lay his head."

[21]Another disciple said to him, "Lord, first let me go and bury my father."

[22]But Jesus told him, "Follow me, and let the dead bury their own dead."

1) Why does Jesus avoid the crowd? Shouldn't he have stayed and taught as many as possible?

2) What does Jesus mean by "let the dead bury their own dead?" Is this a harsh thing to say to someone who just lost his father?

3) We are not told how the two men reacted to the replies from Jesus. Do you think they became disciples? Why or why not?

Day Two Reading and Questions:

[23]Then he got into the boat and his disciples followed him. [24]Without warning, a furious storm came up on the lake, so that the

waves swept over the boat. But Jesus was sleeping. ²⁵The disciples went and woke him, saying, "Lord, save us! We're going to drown!"

²⁶He replied, "You of little faith, why are you so afraid?" Then he got up and rebuked the winds and the waves, and it was completely calm.

²⁷The men were amazed and asked, "What kind of man is this? Even the winds and the waves obey him!"

²⁸When he arrived at the other side in the region of the Gadarenes, two demon-possessed men coming from the tombs met him. They were so violent that no one could pass that way. ²⁹"What do you want with us, Son of God?" they shouted. "Have you come here to torture us before the appointed time?"

³⁰Some distance from them a large herd of pigs was feeding. ³¹The demons begged Jesus, "If you drive us out, send us into the herd of pigs."

³²He said to them, "Go!" So they came out and went into the pigs, and the whole herd rushed down the steep bank into the lake and died in the water. ³³Those tending the pigs ran off, went into the town and reported all this, including what had happened to the demon-possessed men. ³⁴Then the whole town went out to meet Jesus. And when they saw him, they pleaded with him to leave their region.

1) *How did the disciples underestimate the authority of Jesus? Do we ever do the same? Give examples.*

2) *What does the story of the demon-possessed men say about the authority of Jesus?*

3) *Having witnessed a great miracle, why do the townsfolk ask Jesus to leave their region?*

Day Three Reading and Questions:

¹Jesus stepped into a boat, crossed over and came to his own town. ²Some men brought to him a paralytic, lying on a mat. When Jesus saw their faith, he said to the paralytic, "Take heart, son; your sins are forgiven."

³At this, some of the teachers of the law said to themselves, "This fellow is blaspheming!"

⁴Knowing their thoughts, Jesus said, "Why do you entertain evil thoughts in your hearts? ⁵Which is easier: to say, 'Your sins are forgiven,' or to say, 'Get up and walk'? ⁶But so that you may know that the Son of Man has authority on earth to forgive sins...." Then he said to the paralytic, "Get up, take your mat and go home." ⁷And the man got up and went home. ⁸When the crowd saw this, they were filled with awe; and they praised God, who had given such authority to men.

1) Why does Jesus forgive the paralytic before healing him? What is the connection between sickness and sin?

2) Is it significant that this takes place in Jesus' own town? Does that make it more likely or less likely that some will object to Jesus?

3) What authority does Jesus display here?

Day Four Reading and Questions:

⁹As Jesus went on from there, he saw a man named Matthew sitting at the tax collector's booth. "Follow me," he told him, and Matthew got up and followed him.

¹⁰While Jesus was having dinner at Matthew's house, many tax

collectors and "sinners" came and ate with him and his disciples. ¹¹When the Pharisees saw this, they asked his disciples, "Why does your teacher eat with tax collectors and 'sinners'?"

¹²On hearing this, Jesus said, "It is not the healthy who need a doctor, but the sick."

1) What do all those whom Jesus has called to discipleship have in common?

2) Why did they think tax collectors were such big sinners?

3) After all these years, why does the church still spend most of its time and effort with respectable people instead of with sinners?

Day Five Reading and Questions:

Go back and read the entire section.

1) Why do churches try to bring in big crowds when Jesus never calls a crowd to follow him? What does this tell us about the nature of discipleship?

2) What are the different ways that people react to the authority of Jesus in this section? Do we still react in those same ways?

3) What does it take to follow Jesus?

MEDITATIONS ON MATTHEW 8:18-9:13

We try to gain disciples for Jesus in every way possible. Churches have bowling leagues, parenting classes, Christian music festivals, financial success seminars, and all kinds of programs to bring in the crowds.

So why does Jesus avoid crowds? Why does he drive off disciples with strict demands? "Let the dead bury their own dead," who would say such a thing to a grieving son?

Jesus would. Jesus does. He wants him to know the cost of following him. Perhaps Jesus knows something we do not. One cannot call a crowd to discipleship. Each individual must hear the call of Jesus, "Follow me." And it is a call that costs all that we have—our comfortable homes, our families, all our desires for self.

It is a call that requires trust and removes fear. The disciples in the boat have pledged themselves to Jesus, leaving all to follow him. Yet they let their fear get the best of them. They do not trust him to care for them in the storm.

A crowd, a whole town, hears that Jesus has cast demons from two violent men. Do they praise him? Trust him? Follow him? No. They plead with him to leave them alone. You cannot call a crowd to discipleship.

Why not? Why is it even the disciples lack faith? The problem is sin. The paralyzed man has a serious problem. Unable to move, it takes faithful friends to bring him to Jesus. But his greatest problem is not paralysis but sin.

So Jesus forgives. He does not call crowds. He does not call the righteous or the healthy. He calls sinners like Matthew. Like you. Like me. He calls us to trust him in every storm.

"Lord Jesus, forgive. Give us the trust to follow you no matter what it costs. This day may we trust you to deliver us from every evil."

MEDITATIONS

CARING AND CURING
(MATTHEW 9:14-34)

Day One Reading and Questions:

¹⁴Then John's disciples came and asked him, "How is it that we and the Pharisees fast, but your disciples do not fast?"

¹⁵Jesus answered, "How can the guests of the bridegroom mourn while he is with them? The time will come when the bridegroom will be taken from them; then they will fast.

¹⁶"No one sews a patch of unshrunk cloth on an old garment, for the patch will pull away from the garment, making the tear worse. ¹⁷Neither do men pour new wine into old wineskins. If they do, the skins will burst, the wine will run out and the wineskins will be ruined. No, they pour new wine into new wineskins, and both are preserved."

1) Did Jesus and his followers fast? If so, why did Jesus answer the way he did?

2) Who is the bridegroom? When will he be taken away? What is the point of this illustration?

3) What is the point of the new wineskins statement? What are the new wineskins? What implication does this have for how we do church today?

Day Two Reading and Questions:

[18]While he was saying this, a ruler came and knelt before him and said, "My daughter has just died. But come and put your hand on her, and she will live." [19]Jesus got up and went with him, and so did his disciples.

[20]Just then a woman who had been subject to bleeding for twelve years came up behind him and touched the edge of his cloak. [21]She said to herself, "If I only touch his cloak, I will be healed."

[22]Jesus turned and saw her. "Take heart, daughter," he said, "your faith has healed you." And the woman was healed from that moment.

1) What does the ruler believe Jesus can do? Had Jesus done something like this before? What does that say about the ruler's faith?

2) Why do you think the women only wanted to touch Jesus' cloak instead of asking to be healed? What does this say about her faith?

3) Why does Jesus tell the woman to "take heart"? Does she need more than physical healing?

Day Three Reading and Questions:

[23]When Jesus entered the ruler's house and saw the flute players and the noisy crowd, [24]he said, "Go away. The girl is not dead but asleep." But they laughed at him. [25]After the crowd had been put outside, he went in and took the girl by the hand, and she got up. [26]News of this spread through all that region.

1) Why are the flute players and crowd there? Why does Jesus put them outside?

2) Why did the crowd laugh? What does this say about their faith?

3) How does Jesus raise this girl from the dead? How does that make you feel?

Day Four Reading and Questions:

²⁷As Jesus went on from there, two blind men followed him, calling out, "Have mercy on us, Son of David!"
²⁸When he had gone indoors, the blind men came to him, and he asked them, "Do you believe that I am able to do this?"
"Yes, Lord," they replied.
²⁹Then he touched their eyes and said, "According to your faith will it be done to you"; ³⁰and their sight was restored. Jesus warned them sternly, "See that no one knows about this." ³¹But they went out and spread the news about him all over that region.
³²While they were going out, a man who was demon-possessed and could not talk was brought to Jesus. ³³And when the demon was driven out, the man who had been mute spoke. The crowd was amazed and said, "Nothing like this has ever been seen in Israel."
³⁴But the Pharisees said, "It is by the prince of demons that he drives out demons."

1) How does Jesus heal the blind men? What question does he ask them? Has he asked anything like this before?

2) Why does Jesus tell the blind men not to tell of their healing? Why do they tell?

3) Who cannot "see" what Jesus did for the demon-possessed man? Who is really blind in this story? Who is truly mute?

Day Five Reading and Questions:

Go back and read the entire passage.

1) *Notice the way Jesus often touches those whom he heals. What does this say about his care for them? Does it mean more when you are healed by a touch?*

2) *Go back and compare the level of faith in Jesus found in different people in this passage.*

3) *What is the relationship between the "new wineskin" statement and the healings in this passage? What does Jesus do that is so new?*

MEDITATIONS ON MATTHEW 9:14-34

To cure or to care. Which is more important?

When you go to the doctor, do you want someone who is brilliant, skilful, and up-to-date on the latest medical procedures or do you want someone who is gentle and kind, who understands what you are going through?

The answer clearly is "both." We certainly do not want a kind, caring physician who is incompetent, especially if our illness is severe and our life is in his hands. Neither do we want a competent doctor who is harsh, cold, and uncaring.

Jesus is the great physician. He is God among us, a God who cures but also a God who cares. He does not rebuke the woman who tries to touch him secretly. Instead, he speaks to her gently, "take heart, daughter." He raises a little girl from the dead by lovingly taking her by the hand. He softly touches the eyes of the blind and they can see. He opens the mouth of the mute.

But there are those Jesus cannot heal. He does not lack the power. He does not lack the will. He cares for them deeply. But he cannot heal them because they see no need for healing. They criticize Jesus for not fasting. They cannot join in the great wedding feast because they will not join. They want the heady wine of Jesus authority, love, and care to fit in their old wineskins of "that's the way we've always done it."

They are blind. Blinder than the two blind men. Blinder because they cannot see their blindness. Blind because they will not ask for healing. Blind in their distrust of Jesus. So blind that they cannot see the power and loving care of God, they can only see the prince of demons at work.

Are we blind? Can we see the cure and the care Jesus wants to show us? Do we trust him alone to make us whole?

"Lord Jesus, increase our faith. God of love, open our eyes to your work among us. This day may we cry to you for mercy and healing, knowing you hear, touch, and heal."

WORKERS

(MATTHEW 9:35-10:42)

Day One Reading and Questions:

³⁵Jesus went through all the towns and villages, teaching in their synagogues, preaching the good news of the kingdom and healing every disease and sickness. ³⁶When he saw the crowds, he had compassion on them, because they were harassed and helpless, like sheep without a shepherd. ³⁷Then he said to his disciples, "The harvest is plentiful but the workers are few. ³⁸Ask the Lord of the harvest, therefore, to send out workers into his harvest field."

1) How did Jesus show his compassion for the crowds?

2) What does "the harvest is plentiful" mean? How does this relate to the good news of the kingdom?

3) What are the workers Jesus mentioned supposed to do? What is their job? What does it take to get more workers? Who is Lord of the harvest? Is harvesting a divine or a human work?

Day Two Reading and Questions:

¹He called his twelve disciples to him and gave them authority to drive out evil spirits and to heal every disease and sickness.

MEDITATIONS

²These are the names of the twelve apostles: first, Simon (who is called Peter) and his brother Andrew; James son of Zebedee, and his brother John; ³Philip and Bartholomew; Thomas and Matthew the tax collector; James son of Alphaeus, and Thaddaeus; ⁴Simon the Zealot and Judas Iscariot, who betrayed him.

⁵These twelve Jesus sent out with the following instructions: "Do not go among the Gentiles or enter any town of the Samaritans. ⁶Go rather to the lost sheep of Israel. ⁷As you go, preach this message: 'The kingdom of heaven is near.' ⁸Heal the sick, raise the dead, cleanse those who have leprosy, drive out demons. Freely you have received, freely give. ⁹Do not take along any gold or silver or copper in your belts; ¹⁰take no bag for the journey, or extra tunic, or sandals or a staff; for the worker is worth his keep.

¹¹"Whatever town or village you enter, search for some worthy person there and stay at his house until you leave. ¹²As you enter the home, give it your greeting. ¹³If the home is deserving, let your peace rest on it; if it is not, let your peace return to you. ¹⁴If anyone will not welcome you or listen to your words, shake the dust off your feet when you leave that home or town. ¹⁵I tell you the truth, it will be more bearable for Sodom and Gomorrah on the day of judgment than for that town. ¹⁶I am sending you out like sheep among wolves. Therefore be as shrewd as snakes and as innocent as doves."

> 1) Jesus tells the apostles, "Freely have you received, freely give." What had they received? What are they to give?
>
> 2) Why does Jesus tell them to take no money? Who will provide for them?
>
> 3) What does it mean to be shrewd as a snake? How is this different from cynicism?

Day Three Reading and Questions:

¹⁷"Be on your guard against men; they will hand you over to the local councils and flog you in their synagogues. ¹⁸On my account you will be brought before governors and kings as witnesses to them and to the Gentiles. ¹⁹But when they arrest you, do not worry about what to say or how to say it. At that time you will be given what to say, ²⁰for it will not be you speaking, but the Spirit of your Father speaking through you.

²¹"Brother will betray brother to death, and a father his child; children will rebel against their parents and have them put to death. ²²All men will hate you because of me, but he who stands firm to the end will be saved. ²³When you are persecuted in one place, flee to another. I tell you the truth, you will not finish going through the cities of Israel before the Son of Man comes.

²⁴"A student is not above his teacher, nor a servant above his master. ²⁵It is enough for the student to be like his teacher, and the servant like his master. If the head of the house has been called Beelzebub, how much more the members of his household!

²⁶"So do not be afraid of them. There is nothing concealed that will not be disclosed, or hidden that will not be made known. ²⁷What I tell you in the dark, speak in the daylight; what is whispered in your ear, proclaim from the roofs. ²⁸Do not be afraid of those who kill the body but cannot kill the soul. Rather, be afraid of the One who can destroy both soul and body in hell. ²⁹Are not two sparrows sold for a penny? Yet not one of them will fall to the ground apart from the will of your Father. ³⁰And even the very hairs of your head are all numbered. ³¹So don't be afraid; you are worth more than many sparrows."

1) Is the promise of the Spirit speaking through them given only to the apostles or also to us? If to us, have you ever experienced it? What

are the circumstances under which the Spirit speaks in this passage?

2) In what way are the students of Jesus like him in this passage? Do we want to be like Jesus in this way?

3) How many times does Jesus say, "Don't be afraid"? What reasons does he give for their lack of fear?

Day Four Reading and Questions:

³²"Whoever acknowledges me before men, I will also acknowledge him before my Father in heaven. ³³But whoever disowns me before men, I will disown him before my Father in heaven.

³⁴"Do not suppose that I have come to bring peace to the earth. I did not come to bring peace, but a sword. ³⁵For I have come to turn

'a man against his father,
    a daughter against her mother,
a daughter-in-law against her mother-in-law—

    ³⁶a man's enemies will be the members of his own household.'

³⁷"Anyone who loves his father or mother more than me is not worthy of me; anyone who loves his son or daughter more than me is not worthy of me; ³⁸and anyone who does not take his cross and follow me is not worthy of me. ³⁹Whoever finds his life will lose it, and whoever loses his life for my sake will find it.

⁴⁰"He who receives you receives me, and he who receives me receives the one who sent me. ⁴¹Anyone who receives a prophet because he is a prophet will receive a prophet's reward, and anyone who receives a righteous man because he is a righteous man will receive a righteous man's reward. ⁴²And if anyone gives even a cup of cold water to one of these little ones because he is my disciple, I tell you the truth, he will certainly not lose his reward."

1) Jesus came to disrupt households. What does this say about the emphasis on family most churches have? Do we make family an idol?

2) What is the relationship between taking up the cross and loving Jesus more than father, mother, son, or daughter? Can you give an example of someone who had to choose between Jesus and a family member?

3) How will Jesus reward those who receive and care for the apostles? How can we care for those Jesus sends out?

Day Five Reading and Questions:

Go back and read the entire passage.

1) The apostles are given authority to do good—heal, raise the dead, cleans lepers, and drive out demons. Why would anyone oppose those who do good?

2) Why is the good news of the kingdom such bad news to some? Why is the message of Jesus so disruptive politically? Why does it disrupt families?

3) Why are we at times afraid openly to proclaim the message of Jesus? What happens if we do not acknowledge him? What happens to those who follow him? What happens to those who will not follow?

MEDITATIONS ON MATTHEW 9:35-10:42

How should we recruit missionaries? Ads in Christian papers? Through our churches? Displays at Christian colleges? Jesus says to pray. Ask the Lord of the harvest to send forth workers.

How should we support missionaries? Through church agencies? Freewill offerings? Special contributions? Should they work at secular jobs to support themselves? Jesus sends them to the mission field without money, suitcases, or overcoats. He says those they preach to will house and feed them. Or if they do not, God will punish them.

What is the message of the missionary? Here surely we agree with Jesus. The message is "The kingdom of heaven is near." The message is proclaimed not just by word but by actions. The sick are healed, the dead raised, the lepers cleansed, and the demons cast out.

But how can we make people believe the message? How can we be effective missionaries? How can we make converts? Jesus does not seem to be concerned with those questions. The point is to proclaim and show the coming of the kingdom. That kingdom will disrupt other kingdoms. Other kings will bring the missionaries to trial. It will disrupt the religious establishment. They will flog the missionaries in the synagogues. It even will disrupt families, turn father, mother, sister, and brother into enemies.

Is this good news? Yes. But only for those who will surrender to Jesus as their king. Others who disown Jesus will be disowned by him. Their judgment is coming.

Jesus calls us to live out the good news of the kingdom. But we must accept that it is not good news that everyone will accept. Some will fight it and us. We must not fear them. Our job is not to make converts, but to bring in the glorious harvest of God. We pray the Lord of harvest to send more workers, but if we pray this, we must be willing to work ourselves, no matter what the opposition. No matter if government, religion, and family stand against us. By taking up the cross we lose our life and find it. Freely we have received. Freely we must give.

"Lord of the harvest, send forth more workers. Help us today to boldly proclaim the good news of the kingdom, no matter what the cost."

ELIJAH

(MATTHEW 11:1-24)

Day One Reading and Questions:

¹After Jesus had finished instructing his twelve disciples, he went on from there to teach and preach in the towns of Galilee.

²When John heard in prison what Christ was doing, he sent his disciples ³to ask him, "Are you the one who was to come, or should we expect someone else?"

⁴Jesus replied, "Go back and report to John what you hear and see: ⁵The blind receive sight, the lame walk, those who have leprosy are cured, the deaf hear, the dead are raised, and the good news is preached to the poor. ⁶Blessed is the man who does not fall away on account of me."

1) Why did John the Baptist begin to doubt Jesus? Is it wrong to doubt?

2) Why didn't Jesus answer John's question with a "yes" or a "no"? Does Jesus usually answer questions directly? Why not?

3) Why is the good news preached particularly to the poor? Are the poor more righteous? Can rich people receive the good news?

Day Two Reading and Questions:

⁷As John's disciples were leaving, Jesus began to speak to the crowd about John: "What did you go out into the desert to see? A reed swayed by the wind? ⁸If not, what did you go out to see? A man dressed in fine clothes? No, those who wear fine clothes are in kings' palaces. ⁹Then what did you go out to see? A prophet? Yes, I tell you, and more than a prophet. ¹⁰This is the one about whom it is written:
'I will send my messenger ahead of you,
    who will prepare your way before you.'
¹¹I tell you the truth: Among those born of women there has not risen anyone greater than John the Baptist; yet he who is least in the kingdom of heaven is greater than he. ¹²From the days of John the Baptist until now, the kingdom of heaven has been forcefully advancing, and forceful men lay hold of it. ¹³For all the Prophets and the Law prophesied until John. ¹⁴And if you are willing to accept it, he is the Elijah who was to come. ¹⁵He who has ears, let him hear."

1) *What is a prophet? How is John the Baptist a prophet?*

2) *Why is the least in the kingdom greater than John? Do you feel greater than John?*

3) *What are some signs that the kingdom of God is advancing?*

Day Three Reading and Questions:

¹⁶"To what can I compare this generation? They are like children sitting in the marketplaces and calling out to others:
¹⁷'We played the flute for you,

    and you did not dance;
  we sang a dirge
    and you did not mourn.'

[18]For John came neither eating nor drinking, and they say, 'He has a demon.' [19]The Son of Man came eating and drinking, and they say, 'Here is a glutton and a drunkard, a friend of tax collectors and sinners.' But wisdom is proved right by her actions."

1) What do the children in the marketplace want? How is that generation like them? Is our generation like them?

2) Was Jesus a glutton and a drunkard? Why did they make these charges against Jesus?

3) What is the point of "But wisdom is proved right by her actions?"

Day Four Reading and Questions:

[20]Then Jesus began to denounce the cities in which most of his miracles had been performed, because they did not repent. [21]"Woe to you, Korazin! Woe to you, Bethsaida! If the miracles that were performed in you had been performed in Tyre and Sidon, they would have repented long ago in sackcloth and ashes. [22]But I tell you, it will be more bearable for Tyre and Sidon on the day of judgment than for you. [23]And you, Capernaum, will you be lifted up to the skies? No, you will go down to the depths. If the miracles that were performed in you had been performed in Sodom, it would have remained to this day. [24]But I tell you that it will be more bearable for Sodom on the day of judgment than for you."

1) Read the prophecies against Tyre and Sidon in Ezekiel 26 and 27. What were the sins of these cities?

2) Read the story of Sodom in Genesis 19. What were the sins of this city?

3) Why would it be worse for the cities that rejected Jesus?

Day Five Reading and Questions:

Go back and read the entire passage.

1) Jesus condemns the cities that disbelieve but does not criticize John the Baptist for his doubts. What is the difference between doubt and disbelief?

2) Why will some not believe even when they see great miracles?

3) Do we have enough reasons to believe in Jesus? Should we desire more signs and miracles to increase our faith?

MEDITATIONS ON MATTHEW 11:1-24

Belief. Unbelief. Doubt. We meet them all in this passage.

John the Baptist languishes in prison. In that setting doubt comes easily. Why does God leave me in prison? Why am I unjustly punished for proclaiming the good news? Am I really a prophet of God? Is Jesus the one who is to come or did I get it wrong? Is there someone else?

Jesus does not condemn John for his doubts, for John does the right thing with them. He brings them to Jesus. Jesus answers not with a simple, "Yes, I am the one," but with signs that he is the one. Blind see. Lame walk. Lepers are cured. Deaf hear. Dead are raised. The good news is preached to the poor. All the signs of the kingdom are here, present in the work of Jesus.

Doubt comes to all believers. But there is a great difference between doubt and unbelief. John the Baptist had gone into the wilderness as the great prophet, the new Elijah, but not all accepted him. Jesus had done all these great miracles in Korazin, Bethsaida, Capernaum, and other towns, but still some would not repent.

Jesus compares his generation to children who cannot be pleased. Do they want signs? Jesus shows them all kinds of miracles. Do they desire authoritative teaching? Jesus gives it in the Sermon on the Mount. Are they eager for good news? "Repent, for the kingdom is near," say both John and Jesus. Do they want a tough, ascetic religion? John fasts, drinks no wine, and wears camel hair. Do they want a joyous, celebratory religion? Jesus comes eating and drinking with sinners.

What do they want? They don't know. They cannot be pleased, not matter what. Jesus here confronts one of the great mysteries. Why would anyone reject the gracious love of God? Why would anyone throw away the only source of happiness?

But to those who will not come to Jesus, who reject his repeated attempts to gently call them, who will not believe their own eyes or embrace their own happiness, Jesus says, "So be it." It will be more bearable for Sodom on the day of judgment than you.

Jesus here is not judgmental or harsh. Yet his words remind us that following Jesus is serious business. He offers us life. He wants us to reign with him in his kingdom. He wants to make us happy beyond our imaginations. But we must hear his call to follow. He is the one who has come. There will not be another. If we miss Jesus, we miss it all.

"Lord Jesus, help us in our doubts. Increase our faith. May we be content with you. Give us grace to follow you wherever you may lead."

SERVANT AND LORD

(MATTHEW 11:25-12:50)

Day One Reading and Questions:

[25] At that time Jesus said, "I praise you, Father, Lord of heaven and earth, because you have hidden these things from the wise and learned, and revealed them to little children. [26] Yes, Father, for this was your good pleasure.

[27] "All things have been committed to me by my Father. No one knows the Son except the Father, and no one knows the Father except the Son and those to whom the Son chooses to reveal him.

[28] "Come to me, all you who are weary and burdened, and I will give you rest. [29] Take my yoke upon you and learn from me, for I am gentle and humble in heart, and you will find rest for your souls. [30] For my yoke is easy and my burden is light."

1) Does Jesus mean "little children" here literally? Are children the only ones who can understand Jesus? What does Jesus mean here?

2) Does Jesus claim to be the only way to the Father? What are the ways that Christianity is exclusive? How is it inclusive?

3) What is a yoke? Why is the yoke of Jesus easy and light?

Day Two Reading and Questions:

¹At that time Jesus went through the grainfields on the Sabbath. His disciples were hungry and began to pick some heads of grain and eat them. ²When the Pharisees saw this, they said to him, "Look! Your disciples are doing what is unlawful on the Sabbath."

³He answered, "Haven't you read what David did when he and his companions were hungry? ⁴He entered the house of God, and he and his companions ate the consecrated bread—which was not lawful for them to do, but only for the priests. ⁵Or haven't you read in the Law that on the Sabbath the priests in the temple desecrate the day and yet are innocent? ⁶I tell you that one greater than the temple is here. ⁷If you had known what these words mean, 'I desire mercy, not sacrifice,' you would not have condemned the innocent. ⁸For the Son of Man is Lord of the Sabbath."

⁹Going on from that place, he went into their synagogue, ¹⁰and a man with a shriveled hand was there. Looking for a reason to accuse Jesus, they asked him, "Is it lawful to heal on the Sabbath?"

¹¹He said to them, "If any of you has a sheep and it falls into a pit on the Sabbath, will you not take hold of it and lift it out? ¹²How much more valuable is a man than a sheep! Therefore it is lawful to do good on the Sabbath."

¹³Then he said to the man, "Stretch out your hand." So he stretched it out and it was completely restored, just as sound as the other. ¹⁴But the Pharisees went out and plotted how they might kill Jesus.

1) Why was the Sabbath so important to the Pharisees? What were they to do on the Sabbath? How does this relate to what Jesus had just said in Matthew 11:25-30?

2) Why wasn't David punished for breaking the Law? How is mercy more important than sacrifice? How does God judge our obedience?

3) How does Jesus show he is Lord of the Sabbath? What does it mean to be Lord of the Sabbath?

Day Three Reading and Questions:

[15]Aware of this, Jesus withdrew from that place. Many followed him, and he healed all their sick, [16]warning them not to tell who he was. [17]This was to fulfill what was spoken through the prophet Isaiah:

[18]"Here is my servant whom I have chosen,
>   the one I love, in whom I delight;
I will put my Spirit on him,
>   and he will proclaim justice to the nations.
[19]He will not quarrel or cry out;
>   no one will hear his voice in the streets.
[20]A bruised reed he will not break,
>   and a smoldering wick he will not snuff out,
till he leads justice to victory.
>   [21]In his name the nations will put their hope."

[22]Then they brought him a demon-possessed man who was blind and mute, and Jesus healed him, so that he could both talk and see. [23]All the people were astonished and said, "Could this be the Son of David?" [24]But when the Pharisees heard this, they said, "It is only by Beelzebub, the prince of demons, that this fellow drives out demons." [25]Jesus knew their thoughts and said to them, "Every kingdom divided against itself will be ruined, and every city or household divided against itself will not stand. [26]If Satan drives out Satan, he is divided against himself. How then can his kingdom stand? [27]And if I drive out demons by Beelzebub, by whom do your people drive them out? So then, they will be your judges. [28]But if I drive out demons by the Spirit of God, then the kingdom of God has come upon you.

[29]"Or again, how can anyone enter a strong man's house and carry

off his possessions unless he first ties up the strong man? Then he can rob his house.

³⁰"He who is not with me is against me, and he who does not gather with me scatters. ³¹And so I tell you, every sin and blasphemy will be forgiven men, but the blasphemy against the Spirit will not be forgiven. ³²Anyone who speaks a word against the Son of Man will be forgiven, but anyone who speaks against the Holy Spirit will not be forgiven, either in this age or in the age to come.

³³"Make a tree good and its fruit will be good, or make a tree bad and its fruit will be bad, for a tree is recognized by its fruit. ³⁴You brood of vipers, how can you who are evil say anything good? For out of the overflow of the heart the mouth speaks. ³⁵The good man brings good things out of the good stored up in him, and the evil man brings evil things out of the evil stored up in him. ³⁶But I tell you that men will have to give account on the day of judgment for every careless word they have spoken. ³⁷For by your words you will be acquitted, and by your words you will be condemned."

1) How does the quotation from Isaiah picture Jesus as both powerful and gentle?

2) In context, what is speaking against the Holy Spirit? Why will this sin not be forgiven?

3) Are we judged by our actions or our words? What is the connection between them?

Day Four Reading and Questions:

³⁸Then some of the Pharisees and teachers of the law said to him, "Teacher, we want to see a miraculous sign from you."

[39]He answered, "A wicked and adulterous generation asks for a miraculous sign! But none will be given it except the sign of the prophet Jonah. [40]For as Jonah was three days and three nights in the belly of a huge fish, so the Son of Man will be three days and three nights in the heart of the earth. [41]The men of Nineveh will stand up at the judgment with this generation and condemn it; for they repented at the preaching of Jonah, and now one greater than Jonah is here. [42]The Queen of the South will rise at the judgment with this generation and condemn it; for she came from the ends of the earth to listen to Solomon's wisdom, and now one greater than Solomon is here.

[43]"When an evil spirit comes out of a man, it goes through arid places seeking rest and does not find it. [44]Then it says, 'I will return to the house I left.' When it arrives, it finds the house unoccupied, swept clean and put in order. [45]Then it goes and takes with it seven other spirits more wicked than itself, and they go in and live there. And the final condition of that man is worse than the first. That is how it will be with this wicked generation."

[46]While Jesus was still talking to the crowd, his mother and brothers stood outside, wanting to speak to him. [47]Someone told him, "Your mother and brothers are standing outside, wanting to speak to you."

[48]He replied to him, "Who is my mother, and who are my brothers?" [49]Pointing to his disciples, he said, "Here are my mother and my brothers. [50]For whoever does the will of my Father in heaven is my brother and sister and mother."

> 1) Jesus has done many miracles, so why does he refuse to do another for the Pharisees and the teachers of the Law?
>
> 2) Is it enough to be freed from an evil spirit? What should be done after the evil spirit is cast out? How does this relate to the context of this passage?

3) Does Jesus show disrespect to his mother? How are we the family of Jesus? Do you feel like family with Jesus?

Day Five Reading and Questions:

Go back and read the entire passage.

1) What parts of this passage emphasize Jesus as a humble servant? Which ones picture him as a powerful Lord? How can he be both? Do you tend to think of him as servant or Lord?

2) How could the Pharisees believe Jesus was from the devil? If it were Satan empowering Jesus, how would Jesus have behaved differently? How do we know when Satan is at work in us? How do we know when Jesus is?

3) Why do you believe in Jesus? His teaching? His miracles? His life?

MEDITATIONS ON MATTHEW 11:25-12:50

Jesus is Lord.

He is Lord of the universe, God in the flesh, King of Kings, Lord of Lords, ruler of all.

He is even Lord of the Sabbath. The Pharisees rightly worshipped the Lord God as Ruler of all and Giver of the Law. To keep the Law was to give glory to God, so the Pharisees were sticklers when it came to the commandments, especially the Sabbath laws.

And here come the disciples of Jesus, taking a few grains of wheat and eating them as snacks. But to pluck the wheat is work! Work on the Sabbath! Why would Jesus who claims to keep the Law allow his disciples to break the Sabbath command. Doesn't Jesus have respect for the Lord God?

When confronted by the Pharisees, Jesus defends his disciples in a startling way. He doesn't explain that picking a few grains is not work. He doesn't debate the meaning of the Sabbath laws. Instead, he brings up what must have been an embarrassing biblical story to the Pharisees. What about David? Did he not clearly break the law by eating the consecrated bread? Yet God never condemns David for this act.

Then Jesus makes an even more shocking claim. "For the Son of Man is Lord of the Sabbath." In essence, Jesus is saying, "I am the Lord God. I made the Law. I cannot break the Law because I am greater than the Law."

To prove his point he then intentionally heals a man on the Sabbath. He rubs the noses of the Pharisees in the question of his identity. He claims to be God. They plot to kill him. They cannot accept him as Lord so they explain his power as demonic, calling God the devil. Such speech against the Holy Spirit who inhabits Jesus cannot be forgiven. The Pharisees are so blind they will not see. Miracles are happening all around them and still they ask for signs.

Who is Jesus? He is Lord. Lawgiver. Ruler. King. But he also is the one who came to serve. He offers to give us rest, pulling the yoke beside us to make it easy and light. He is the gentle servant who brings good news. He is the one who invites us into his family.

Who is Jesus to you? An overly familiar name? A religious figure? Is he your Lord? Your brother? The one who serves and works beside you?

"Brother Jesus, you are our Lord and ruler. You are our servant. This day, may you be in us and with us. Give us grace to worship, to be served, and to follow."

TRUE VALUE

(MATTHEW 13:1-58)

Day One Reading and Questions:

¹That same day Jesus went out of the house and sat by the lake. ²Such large crowds gathered around him that he got into a boat and sat in it, while all the people stood on the shore. ³Then he told them many things in parables, saying: "A farmer went out to sow his seed. ⁴As he was scattering the seed, some fell along the path, and the birds came and ate it up. ⁵Some fell on rocky places, where it did not have much soil. It sprang up quickly, because the soil was shallow. ⁶But when the sun came up, the plants were scorched, and they withered because they had no root. ⁷Other seed fell among thorns, which grew up and choked the plants. ⁸Still other seed fell on good soil, where it produced a crop—a hundred, sixty or thirty times what was sown. ⁹He who has ears, let him hear."

¹⁰The disciples came to him and asked, "Why do you speak to the people in parables?"

¹¹He replied, "The knowledge of the secrets of the kingdom of heaven has been given to you, but not to them. ¹²Whoever has will be given more, and he will have an abundance. Whoever does not have, even what he has will be taken from him. ¹³This is why I speak to them in parables:

'Though seeing, they do not see;
    though hearing, they do not hear or understand.'

[14]"In them is fulfilled the prophecy of Isaiah:

'You will be ever hearing but never understanding;
    you will be ever seeing but never perceiving.
[15]For this people's heart has become calloused;
    they hardly hear with their ears,
    and they have closed their eyes.
Otherwise they might see with their eyes,
    hear with their ears,
    understand with their hearts
    and turn, and I would heal them.'

[16]But blessed are your eyes because they see, and your ears because they hear. [17]For I tell you the truth, many prophets and righteous men longed to see what you see but did not see it, and to hear what you hear but did not hear it.

[18]"Listen then to what the parable of the sower means: [19]When anyone hears the message about the kingdom and does not understand it, the evil one comes and snatches away what was sown in his heart. This is the seed sown along the path. [20]The one who received the seed that fell on rocky places is the man who hears the word and at once receives it with joy. [21]But since he has no root, he lasts only a short time. When trouble or persecution comes because of the word, he quickly falls away. [22]The one who received the seed that fell among the thorns is the man who hears the word, but the worries of this life and the deceitfulness of wealth choke it, making it unfruitful. [23]But the one who received the seed that fell on good soil is the man who hears the word and understands it. He produces a crop, yielding a hundred, sixty or thirty times what was sown."

1) Why did Jesus speak in parables? Did he want some people not to understand him? Why?

2) What does it take to receive the seed or word?

3) *Why do you think this is the first parable in Matthew? How does this parable introduce the others? How is this a parable about hearing parables?*

Day Two Reading and Questions:

[24]Jesus told them another parable: "The kingdom of heaven is like a man who sowed good seed in his field. [25]But while everyone was sleeping, his enemy came and sowed weeds among the wheat, and went away. [26]When the wheat sprouted and formed heads, then the weeds also appeared.

[27]"The owner's servants came to him and said, 'Sir, didn't you sow good seed in your field? Where then did the weeds come from?'

[28]'An enemy did this,' he replied.

"The servants asked him, 'Do you want us to go and pull them up?'

[29]'No,' he answered, 'because while you are pulling the weeds, you may root up the wheat with them. [30]Let both grow together until the harvest. At that time I will tell the harvesters: First collect the weeds and tie them in bundles to be burned; then gather the wheat and bring it into my barn.' "

[31]He told them another parable: "The kingdom of heaven is like a mustard seed, which a man took and planted in his field. [32]Though it is the smallest of all your seeds, yet when it grows, it is the largest of garden plants and becomes a tree, so that the birds of the air come and perch in its branches."

[33]He told them still another parable: "The kingdom of heaven is like yeast that a woman took and mixed into a large amount of flour until it worked all through the dough."

[34]Jesus spoke all these things to the crowd in parables; he did not say anything to them without using a parable. [35]So was fulfilled what was spoken through the prophet:

"I will open my mouth in parables,
 I will utter things hidden since the creation of the world."

³⁶Then he left the crowd and went into the house. His disciples came to him and said, "Explain to us the parable of the weeds in the field."

³⁷He answered, "The one who sowed the good seed is the Son of Man. ³⁸The field is the world, and the good seed stands for the sons of the kingdom. The weeds are the sons of the evil one, ³⁹and the enemy who sows them is the devil. The harvest is the end of the age, and the harvesters are angels.

⁴⁰"As the weeds are pulled up and burned in the fire, so it will be at the end of the age. ⁴¹The Son of Man will send out his angels, and they will weed out of his kingdom everything that causes sin and all who do evil. ⁴²They will throw them into the fiery furnace, where there will be weeping and gnashing of teeth. ⁴³Then the righteous will shine like the sun in the kingdom of their Father. He who has ears, let him hear."

1) Why does Jesus explain the parable of the weeds? Isn't the meaning obvious?

2) Why doesn't God separate the weeds from the wheat now? What does that say about how we should judge others?

3) What is the point of the parables of the mustard seed and the yeast? Why doesn't Jesus explain them?

Day Three Reading and Questions:

⁴⁴"The kingdom of heaven is like treasure hidden in a field. When a man found it, he hid it again, and then in his joy went and sold all he

had and bought that field.

⁴⁵"Again, the kingdom of heaven is like a merchant looking for fine pearls. ⁴⁶When he found one of great value, he went away and sold everything he had and bought it.

⁴⁷"Once again, the kingdom of heaven is like a net that was let down into the lake and caught all kinds of fish. ⁴⁸When it was full, the fishermen pulled it up on the shore. Then they sat down and collected the good fish in baskets, but threw the bad away. ⁴⁹This is how it will be at the end of the age. The angels will come and separate the wicked from the righteous ⁵⁰and throw them into the fiery furnace, where there will be weeping and gnashing of teeth.

⁵¹"Have you understood all these things?" Jesus asked.

"Yes," they replied.

⁵²He said to them, "Therefore every teacher of the law who has been instructed about the kingdom of heaven is like the owner of a house who brings out of his storeroom new treasures as well as old."

1) What is the meaning of the parables of the hidden treasure and the pearl?

2) The parable of the fish in the net is like what other parable in this section? Why does Jesus tell similar parables?

3) What is the point of the statement about "new treasures and old"? What are the new treasures? What are the old?

Day Four Reading and Questions:

⁵³When Jesus had finished these parables, he moved on from there. ⁵⁴Coming to his hometown, he began teaching the people in their synagogue, and they were amazed. "Where did this man get this

wisdom and these miraculous powers?" they asked. [55]"Isn't this the carpenter's son? Isn't his mother's name Mary, and aren't his brothers James, Joseph, Simon and Judas? [56]Aren't all his sisters with us? Where then did this man get all these things?" [57]And they took offense at him.

But Jesus said to them, "Only in his hometown and in his own house is a prophet without honor."

[58]And he did not do many miracles there because of their lack of faith.

> 1) Why were his hometown folks offended at Jesus?
>
> 2) Are we ever offended or embarrassed at Jesus? Give examples.
>
> 3) What is the connection between miracles and faith? Does faith have to be present for miracles to occur?

Day Five Reading and Questions:

Go back and read the entire passage.

> 1) Jesus does not make it easy for people to understand his teaching. Should we make it easy? What is the danger of making Jesus' teachings too easy to understand?
>
> 2) What theme do all of these parables have in common?
>
> 3) Is it possible to think we have Jesus all figured out only to miss him completely? Isn't that what his hometown people did? How can we avoid being too familiar with Jesus?

MEDITATIONS ON MATTHEW 13:1-58

True value. That's what we want out of every product we buy. But we don't always get it. All of us have fallen for the hype and bought junk.

Missing true value is more of a tragedy in life. We search for what is real, what gives life meaning, and what will make us happy. What is so valuable that we will give all, sell all, and risk all to have it?

That's the question Jesus raises in these parables. They are all parables of judgment, not just the final day of judgment, but judging what is truly valuable. True value cannot always be seen at first. It may start small like a seed or yeast and then grow into something of great value. On the other hand, true value is sometimes as obvious as a treasure or a pearl. Sometimes what has value is mixed with the worthless—like weeds and wheat, like good and bad fish in a net—and cannot be separated until the end of the age.

So how can we find what is truly valuable? We must have good hearts that accept the gift of the seed or word of God. And what does that seed or word reveal? What is of infinite value, so much so that it demands all that we have? It is the amazing Jesus himself. The question is, will we truly recognize this treasure or will be offended at him? Like his hometown folk, will our own familiarity with Jesus blind us to his true value?

"Jesus, we call your name so often, we praise you in song, we even hear your name used in vain. Open our hearts to see what a treasure you are. Do not let us miss you because we think we know you so well."

DON'T BE AFRAID

(MATTHEW 14:1-15:20)

Day One Reading and Questions:

¹At that time Herod the tetrarch heard the reports about Jesus, ²and he said to his attendants, "This is John the Baptist; he has risen from the dead! That is why miraculous powers are at work in him."

³Now Herod had arrested John and bound him and put him in prison because of Herodias, his brother Philip's wife, ⁴for John had been saying to him: "It is not lawful for you to have her." ⁵Herod wanted to kill John, but he was afraid of the people, because they considered him a prophet.

⁶On Herod's birthday the daughter of Herodias danced for them and pleased Herod so much ⁷that he promised with an oath to give her whatever she asked. ⁸Prompted by her mother, she said, "Give me here on a platter the head of John the Baptist." ⁹The king was distressed, but because of his oaths and his dinner guests, he ordered that her request be granted ¹⁰and had John beheaded in the prison. ¹¹His head was brought in on a platter and given to the girl, who carried it to her mother. ¹²John's disciples came and took his body and buried it. Then they went and told Jesus.

1) Why does Herod think Jesus is John the Baptist raised from the dead?

2) Why did killing John distress Herod?

3) Why did Herod kill John? What factors today influence us to go against our consciences?

Day Two Reading and Questions:

[13]When Jesus heard what had happened, he withdrew by boat privately to a solitary place. Hearing of this, the crowds followed him on foot from the towns. [14]When Jesus landed and saw a large crowd, he had compassion on them and healed their sick.

[15]As evening approached, the disciples came to him and said, "This is a remote place, and it's already getting late. Send the crowds away, so they can go to the villages and buy themselves some food."

[16]Jesus replied, "They do not need to go away. You give them something to eat."

[17]"We have here only five loaves of bread and two fish," they answered.

[18]"Bring them here to me," he said. [19]And he directed the people to sit down on the grass. Taking the five loaves and the two fish and looking up to heaven, he gave thanks and broke the loaves. Then he gave them to the disciples, and the disciples gave them to the people. [20]They all ate and were satisfied, and the disciples picked up twelve basketfuls of broken pieces that were left over. [21]The number of those who ate was about five thousand men, besides women and children.

1) What causes Jesus to withdraw to a solitary place with his disciples? What prevents them from being alone?

2) What are two ways Jesus shows compassion to the crowd?

3) Why does Jesus tell the disciples to feed the crowd? What does their response say about their faith?

Day Three Reading and Questions:

²²Immediately Jesus made the disciples get into the boat and go on ahead of him to the other side, while he dismissed the crowd. ²³After he had dismissed them, he went up on a mountainside by himself to pray. When evening came, he was there alone, ²⁴but the boat was already a considerable distance from land, buffeted by the waves because the wind was against it.

²⁵During the fourth watch of the night Jesus went out to them, walking on the lake. ²⁶When the disciples saw him walking on the lake, they were terrified. "It's a ghost," they said, and cried out in fear.

²⁷But Jesus immediately said to them: "Take courage! It is I. Don't be afraid."

²⁸"Lord, if it's you," Peter replied, "tell me to come to you on the water."

²⁹"Come," he said.

³⁰Then Peter got down out of the boat, walked on the water and came toward Jesus. But when he saw the wind, he was afraid and, beginning to sink, cried out, "Lord, save me!"

³¹Immediately Jesus reached out his hand and caught him. "You of little faith," he said, "why did you doubt?"

³²And when they climbed into the boat, the wind died down. ³³Then those who were in the boat worshiped him, saying, "Truly you are the Son of God."

³⁴When they had crossed over, they landed at Gennesaret. ³⁵And when the men of that place recognized Jesus, they sent word to all the surrounding country. People brought all their sick to him ³⁶and begged him to let the sick just touch the edge of his cloak, and all who touched him were healed.

1) Why does Jesus send the disciples away and then dismiss the crowd? How does this show what is important to Jesus?

2) What part does fear play in the story of walking on water? How does fear keep us from seeing and following Jesus?

3) After seeing all of Jesus' miracles, why does this one make the disciples respond with, "Truly, you are the Son of God"? Does this have anything to do with the occupation of many of the disciples?

Day Four Reading and Questions:

¹Then some Pharisees and teachers of the law came to Jesus from Jerusalem and asked, ²"Why do your disciples break the tradition of the elders? They don't wash their hands before they eat!"

³Jesus replied, "And why do you break the command of God for the sake of your tradition? ⁴For God said, 'Honor your father and mother' and 'Anyone who curses his father or mother must be put to death.' ⁵But you say that if a man says to his father or mother, 'Whatever help you might otherwise have received from me is a gift devoted to God,' ⁶he is not to 'honor his father' with it. Thus you nullify the word of God for the sake of your tradition. ⁷You hypocrites! Isaiah was right when he prophesied about you:

⁸"These people honor me with their lips,
> but their hearts are far from me.

⁹They worship me in vain;
> their teachings are but rules taught by men.'"

¹⁰Jesus called the crowd to him and said, "Listen and understand. ¹¹What goes into a man's mouth does not make him 'unclean,' but what comes out of his mouth, that is what makes him 'unclean.'"

¹²Then the disciples came to him and asked, "Do you know that the Pharisees were offended when they heard this?"

¹³He replied, "Every plant that my heavenly Father has not planted will be pulled up by the roots. ¹⁴Leave them; they are blind guides. If a

blind man leads a blind man, both will fall into a pit."

¹⁵Peter said, "Explain the parable to us."

¹⁶"Are you still so dull?" Jesus asked them. ¹⁷"Don't you see that whatever enters the mouth goes into the stomach and then out of the body? ¹⁸But the things that come out of the mouth come from the heart, and these make a man 'unclean.' ¹⁹For out of the heart come evil thoughts, murder, adultery, sexual immorality, theft, false testimony, slander. ²⁰These are what make a man 'unclean'; but eating with unwashed hands does not make him 'unclean.'"

> 1) Why are the disciples afraid to offend the Pharisees? Is Jesus afraid? Should we always be afraid of offending someone?
>
> 2) Were the Pharisees and the teachers of the Law really concerned with keeping the Law of God? Why or why not?
>
> 3) What does Jesus mean by "heart"? Why is the heart important in our relationship with God?

Day Five Reading and Questions:

Go back and read the entire passage.

> 1) How does fear affect Herod in this passage?
>
> 2) How does fear affect the disciples?
>
> 3) What are the Pharisees afraid of? List the ways Jesus overcomes fear in this section.

MEDITATIONS ON MATTHEW 14:1-15:20

Fear.

Fear can paralyze evils actions and good ones. Herod wants to kill John the Baptist, but fear of public opinion stops him. When he makes his rash promise to the daughter of Herodias, her desire for John's death would seem to be what Herod himself wants. But Herod is caught between fears. He is afraid of John's popularity but also afraid of losing face and appearing foolish before his birthday guests. His fear leads to the death of a righteous man.

Fear can lead to no action at all. The disciples are afraid that the people are hungry, afraid that they do not have enough to feed them. Jesus takes the little they give him and feeds the multitude. Don't we often have the same fear as the disciples, the fear of not having enough? There is no reason to fear hunger or any human need while Jesus is around.

Fear can even blind disciples to Jesus. Because of fear, they do not recognize him walking on the water. Fear overcomes Peter's faith and he sinks beneath the waves. Do we sometimes fear the unexpected actions of Jesus? Are we willing to step out on the water? Do we trust Jesus or fear the wind and the waves?

The Pharisees thrive on fear. Fear that someone else (not themselves) might be breaking the Law. Fear that standards are not being kept, fear of a permissive attitude, most of all fear of a genuine relationship with God and others. Even honoring parents is a law to them (a law they technically, but not really keep), not a loving relationship. Strangely enough, the disciples are more afraid of offending the Pharisees than they are of offending Jesus.

Jesus banishes fear. Fear of popular opinion. Fear of appearing foolish. Fear of not having enough. He even banishes that deep fear expressed in the legalism of the Pharisees, the fear of not being right with God. Fear that comes from a bad heart. How does he overcome fear? By calling us to trust him. To trust him for food. To trust him for protection from the storm. To trust him to make our hearts right with God, not through tradition or legalism, but by his power. Truly he is the Son of God.

"Lord Jesus, forgive our little faith. Give us hearts that trust you in hunger, storm, and even death. May our obedience to you be genuinely from those good hearts."

BREAD

(MATTHEW 15:21-16:12)

Day One Reading and Questions:

²¹Leaving that place, Jesus withdrew to the region of Tyre and Sidon. ²²A Canaanite woman from that vicinity came to him, crying out, "Lord, Son of David, have mercy on me! My daughter is suffering terribly from demon-possession."

²³Jesus did not answer a word. So his disciples came to him and urged him, "Send her away, for she keeps crying out after us."

²⁴He answered, "I was sent only to the lost sheep of Israel."

²⁵The woman came and knelt before him. "Lord, help me!" she said.

²⁶He replied, "It is not right to take the children's bread and toss it to their dogs."

²⁷"Yes, Lord," she said, "but even the dogs eat the crumbs that fall from their masters' table."

²⁸Then Jesus answered, "Woman, you have great faith! Your request is granted." And her daughter was healed from that very hour.

1) Why didn't Jesus answer the woman at first? Is he rude to her? Unfeeling?

2) Why does Jesus call her a dog? Is this rude or lacking in compassion?

3) How does the woman show her great faith? Must we be persistent to receive blessings from Jesus? Why? Doesn't he want to give to us?

Day Two Reading and Questions:

[29] Jesus left there and went along the Sea of Galilee. Then he went up on a mountainside and sat down. [30] Great crowds came to him, bringing the lame, the blind, the crippled, the mute and many others, and laid them at his feet; and he healed them. [31] The people were amazed when they saw the mute speaking, the crippled made well, the lame walking and the blind seeing. And they praised the God of Israel.

[32] Jesus called his disciples to him and said, "I have compassion for these people; they have already been with me three days and have nothing to eat. I do not want to send them away hungry, or they may collapse on the way."

[33] His disciples answered, "Where could we get enough bread in this remote place to feed such a crowd?"

[34] "How many loaves do you have?" Jesus asked.

"Seven," they replied, "and a few small fish."

[35] He told the crowd to sit down on the ground. [36] Then he took the seven loaves and the fish, and when he had given thanks, he broke them and gave them to the disciples, and they in turn to the people. [37] They all ate and were satisfied. Afterward the disciples picked up seven basketfuls of broken pieces that were left over. [38] The number of those who ate was four thousand, besides women and children. [39] After Jesus had sent the crowd away, he got into the boat and went to the vicinity of Magadan.

1) Why do the disciples wonder where to find bread to feed the crowd? Did they not witness the feeding of the 5000?

2) Why does Jesus repeat his feeding miracle, first 5000, then 4000? What is the point of the miracle?

3) What are ways Jesus shows compassion to the crowd?

Day Three Reading and Questions:

¹The Pharisees and Sadducees came to Jesus and tested him by asking him to show them a sign from heaven.
²He replied, "When evening comes, you say, 'It will be fair weather, for the sky is red,' ³and in the morning, 'Today it will be stormy, for the sky is red and overcast.' You know how to interpret the appearance of the sky, but you cannot interpret the signs of the times. ⁴A wicked and adulterous generation looks for a miraculous sign, but none will be given it except the sign of Jonah." Jesus then left them and went away.

1) Does asking for a sign show faith? Are we more apt to believe in Jesus if we see miracles?

2) What is the point of Jesus' weather example?

3) What is the sign of Jonah?

Day Four Reading and Questions:

⁵When they went across the lake, the disciples forgot to take bread. ⁶"Be careful," Jesus said to them. "Be on your guard against the yeast of the Pharisees and Sadducees."
⁷They discussed this among themselves and said, "It is because we didn't bring any bread."
⁸Aware of their discussion, Jesus asked, "You of little faith, why are you talking among yourselves about having no bread? ⁹Do you still not understand? Don't you remember the five loaves for the five thousand, and how many basketfuls you gathered? ¹⁰Or the seven loaves for the

four thousand, and how many basketfuls you gathered? [11]How is it you don't understand that I was not talking to you about bread? But be on your guard against the yeast of the Pharisees and Sadducees." [12]Then they understood that he was not telling them to guard against the yeast used in bread, but against the teaching of the Pharisees and Sadducees.

1) *What is yeast? What does it do? How is the teaching of the Pharisees and Sadducees like yeast?*

2) *Why are the disciples worried about bread? Why do they have "little faith"?*

3) *How does this passage relate to the request for signs?*

Day Five Reading and Questions:

Go back and read the entire passage.

1) *List the ways the word "bread" is used in this passage.*

2) *Are the two feeding miracles about more than literal bread? What other things does Jesus feed his followers?*

3) *How does bread relate to signs in this passage?*

MEDITATIONS ON MATTHEW 15:21-16:12

I just ordered a sandwich on pecan raspberry bread. It sounded strange and wonderful. Of all the many foods I like, few are better than warm bread, straight from the oven with that unmistakable yeasty smell. For many in the world, daily bread is precisely that. It is bread or nothing. Bread means food and food means anything that satisfies our deepest longings.

There's a woman who needs more than food. Her daughter is demon-possessed. Frantic for help, she comes to Jesus. He ignores her. Then he talks about bread and calls her a dog. "It is not right to take the children's bread and toss it to the dogs." Why would Jesus say such a thing? Because the woman is not a Jew but a Canaanite, a descendent of those who fought and murdered God's people.

So how does the woman react? "Even the dogs eat the crumbs that fall from their master's table." Jesus praises her for her faith and heals her daughter.

Is Jesus a bigot? Prejudiced against non-Jews? I don't think so. Matthew tells us that non-Jews, the Magi, are the first to worship him. So why is Jesus so harsh toward this woman? I think he wanted to know how hungry she was. How much did she want the bread of healing?

Later, for the second time Jesus faces a hungry crowd. Hungry for healing, for teaching, and for bread. Out of compassion he feeds 4000 of them with seven loaves and few fish. Jesus always has more than enough bread.

But some cannot see his bread. They refuse to taste his healing, his teaching, and his compassion. Jesus warns against the yeast of the Pharisees and Sadducees. The disciples have literal bread on their minds. Instead Jesus is warning against those who make their own bread, insisting on their own teachings, traditions, and understandings instead of being hungry for the bread of Christ.

Are we hungry? Hungry for healing, for teaching, for compassion? Or, like the Pharisees and Sadducees, do we refuse the bread Jesus provides? Do we constantly ask him for new signs, asking, "What have you done for me lately?" Are we willing to humbly receive even the crumbs he provides? If we come in faith, his compassion is boundless. He feeds us with the bread that satisfies.

"Lord Jesus, forgive us for hungering after the wrong things. May our own understandings and teachings never keep us from trusting in you."

MEDITATIONS

REVELATION
(MATTHEW 16:13-17:23)

Day One Reading and Questions:

¹³When Jesus came to the region of Caesarea Philippi, he asked his disciples, "Who do people say the Son of Man is?"

¹⁴They replied, "Some say John the Baptist; others say Elijah; and still others, Jeremiah or one of the prophets."

¹⁵"But what about you?" he asked. "Who do you say I am?"

¹⁶Simon Peter answered, "You are the Christ, the Son of the living God."

¹⁷Jesus replied, "Blessed are you, Simon son of Jonah, for this was not revealed to you by man, but by my Father in heaven. ¹⁸And I tell you that you are Peter, and on this rock I will build my church, and the gates of Hades will not overcome it. ¹⁹I will give you the keys of the kingdom of heaven; whatever you bind on earth will be bound in heaven, and whatever you loose on earth will be loosed in heaven." ²⁰Then he warned his disciples not to tell anyone that he was the Christ.

1) What does Jesus mean when he says the Father revealed this to Peter? How does God the Father reveal Jesus to us?

2) What is the rock on which the church is built? Since Peter means "rock," is the church built on Peter?

3) Why does Jesus warn the disciples not to tell that he is the Messiah? Shouldn't they evangelize?

Day Two Reading and Questions:

²¹From that time on Jesus began to explain to his disciples that he must go to Jerusalem and suffer many things at the hands of the elders, chief priests and teachers of the law, and that he must be killed and on the third day be raised to life.

²²Peter took him aside and began to rebuke him. "Never, Lord!" he said. "This shall never happen to you!"

²³Jesus turned and said to Peter, "Get behind me, Satan! You are a stumbling block to me; you do not have in mind the things of God, but the things of men."

²⁴Then Jesus said to his disciples, "If anyone would come after me, he must deny himself and take up his cross and follow me. ²⁵For whoever wants to save his life will lose it, but whoever loses his life for me will find it. ²⁶What good will it be for a man if he gains the whole world, yet forfeits his soul? Or what can a man give in exchange for his soul? ²⁷For the Son of Man is going to come in his Father's glory with his angels, and then he will reward each person according to what he has done. ²⁸I tell you the truth, some who are standing here will not taste death before they see the Son of Man coming in his kingdom."

1) Why does Peter rebuke Jesus? Why can't Peter accept a suffering and dying Messiah?

2) Why does Jesus rebuke Peter so strongly? How is Peter like Satan?

3) What does it mean to take up the cross? What does it mean to lose our lives for Jesus?

Day Three Reading and Questions:

¹After six days Jesus took with him Peter, James and John the brother of James, and led them up a high mountain by themselves. ²There he was transfigured before them. His face shone like the sun, and his clothes became as white as the light. ³Just then there appeared before them Moses and Elijah, talking with Jesus.

⁴Peter said to Jesus, "Lord, it is good for us to be here. If you wish, I will put up three shelters—one for you, one for Moses and one for Elijah."

⁵While he was still speaking, a bright cloud enveloped them, and a voice from the cloud said, "This is my Son, whom I love; with him I am well pleased. Listen to him!"

⁶When the disciples heard this, they fell facedown to the ground, terrified. ⁷But Jesus came and touched them. "Get up," he said. "Don't be afraid." ⁸When they looked up, they saw no one except Jesus.

⁹As they were coming down the mountain, Jesus instructed them, "Don't tell anyone what you have seen, until the Son of Man has been raised from the dead."

¹⁰The disciples asked him, "Why then do the teachers of the law say that Elijah must come first?"

¹¹Jesus replied, "To be sure, Elijah comes and will restore all things. ¹²But I tell you, Elijah has already come, and they did not recognize him, but have done to him everything they wished. In the same way the Son of Man is going to suffer at their hands." ¹³Then the disciples understood that he was talking to them about John the Baptist.

1) How does this story relate to the promise of Jesus in Matthew 16:28?

2) What do Moses, Elijah, and Jesus have in common?

3) What is the significance of the voice from the cloud?

Day Four Readings and Questions:

¹⁴When they came to the crowd, a man approached Jesus and knelt before him. ¹⁵"Lord, have mercy on my son," he said. "He has seizures and is suffering greatly. He often falls into the fire or into the water. ¹⁶I brought him to your disciples, but they could not heal him."

¹⁷"O unbelieving and perverse generation," Jesus replied, "how long shall I stay with you? How long shall I put up with you? Bring the boy here to me." ¹⁸Jesus rebuked the demon, and it came out of the boy, and he was healed from that moment.

¹⁹Then the disciples came to Jesus in private and asked, "Why couldn't we drive it out?"

²⁰He replied, "Because you have so little faith. I tell you the truth, if you have faith as small as a mustard seed, you can say to this mountain, 'Move from here to there' and it will move. Nothing will be impossible for you."

²²When they came together in Galilee, he said to them, "The Son of Man is going to be betrayed into the hands of men. ²³They will kill him, and on the third day he will be raised to life." And the disciples were filled with grief.

1) Why do you think the disciples lacked faith? Why is Jesus so exasperated by their lack of faith.

2) Can faith literally move mountains? What does Jesus mean by saying it can?

3) Why are the disciples filled with grief? What part of Jesus prediction do they seem to fail to hear?

Day Five Readings and Questions:

Go back and read the entire passage.

1) In light of all Jesus had done, why does it take the disciples so long to recognize him as Messiah? What is God's part in furthering that recognition?

2) Is it easier to believe in a glorious, transfigured Jesus or in a suffering and dying Messiah? Is a dead Messiah a failure? Why did Peter think so? Why didn't the disciples understand about the resurrection?

3) List the ways the disciples show their unbelief in this section.

MEDITATIONS ON MATTHEW 16:13-17:23

It's so easy to believe in Jesus. He teaches with authority, unlike anyone else. He casts out demons. He heals the sick. He shows amazing compassion. Why would anyone not believe in him?

But Jesus says some things that are hard to believe. "Deny yourself." "Take up the cross." "Whoever loses his life for me will find it." Who wants to die? Who willingly embraces failure? Who wants to be tortured on a cross?

Jesus does. He never asks us to do what he is unwilling to do himself. He is willing to suffer and die, knowing that is not the end of the story. There is resurrection, life, and glory.

The disciples do not get it. Do we? Do we not want exactly what those disciples wanted, a triumphant and successful Messiah? When Peter finally confesses that Jesus is the long-awaited Savior, no doubt his imagination is fired with visions of sharing in the triumph, glory, and honor the Messiah will bring. What Peter and we cannot fathom is the depths of degradation and suffering we must go through with Jesus to get there.

Following Jesus is about success, triumph, and glory. Three of the disciples even gain a glimpse of that glory on the mountain of transfiguration. But the path to glory is through failure, loss, and shame. It is all about death and resurrection.

Which calls for great trust, a faith that can move mountains. Just like these disciples, we must trust that resurrection awaits us after death. We must trust that lives of self-denial and suffering are ultimately not failure but success. Only in this daily trust can we truly follow Jesus and have the power to show his compassion to those in need.

"Lord Jesus, may we see you clearly today as Messiah, as glorious Lord, and as Suffering Servant. Give us trust in the power of resurrection. Give us faith to move mountains of fear, pain, and ignorance."

MEDITATIONS

KINGDOM
(MATTHEW 17:24-18:35)

Day One Readings and Questions:

²⁴After Jesus and his disciples arrived in Capernaum, the collectors of the two-drachma tax came to Peter and asked, "Doesn't your teacher pay the temple tax?"

²⁵"Yes, he does," he replied.

When Peter came into the house, Jesus was the first to speak. "What do you think, Simon?" he asked. "From whom do the kings of the earth collect duty and taxes—from their own sons or from others?"

²⁶"From others," Peter answered.

²⁷"Then the sons are exempt," Jesus said to him. "But so that we may not offend them, go to the lake and throw out your line. Take the first fish you catch; open its mouth and you will find a four-drachma coin. Take it and give it to them for my tax and yours."

1) Does Jesus owe this tax? Why or why not? If he does not owe it, why does he pay it?

2) What does Jesus mean about the sons being exempt? Are Christians exempt from taxes? Where is our citizenship?

3) What does this passage imply about the kingdom Jesus is bringing? What is the relationship between that kingdom and earthly kingdoms?

Day Two Readings and Questions:

¹At that time the disciples came to Jesus and asked, "Who is the greatest in the kingdom of heaven?"

²He called a little child and had him stand among them. ³And he said: "I tell you the truth, unless you change and become like little children, you will never enter the kingdom of heaven. ⁴Therefore, whoever humbles himself like this child is the greatest in the kingdom of heaven.

⁵"And whoever welcomes a little child like this in my name welcomes me. ⁶But if anyone causes one of these little ones who believe in me to sin, it would be better for him to have a large millstone hung around his neck and to be drowned in the depths of the sea.

⁷"Woe to the world because of the things that cause people to sin! Such things must come, but woe to the man through whom they come! ⁸If your hand or your foot causes you to sin, cut it off and throw it away. It is better for you to enter life maimed or crippled than to have two hands or two feet and be thrown into eternal fire. ⁹And if your eye causes you to sin, gouge it out and throw it away. It is better for you to enter life with one eye than to have two eyes and be thrown into the fire of hell."

1) How are children humble? Does this refer to their attitude or to their status in society?

2) How important is it to protect children? Why is it so terrible to cause them to sin?

3) Would cutting off hands, feet, and eyes keep us from sinning? Isn't sin a matter of the heart? What does Jesus mean by talking about cutting off body parts?

Day Three Readings and Questions:

[10]"See that you do not look down on one of these little ones. For I tell you that their angels in heaven always see the face of my Father in heaven.

[12]"What do you think? If a man owns a hundred sheep, and one of them wanders away, will he not leave the ninety-nine on the hills and go to look for the one that wandered off? [13]And if he finds it, I tell you the truth, he is happier about that one sheep than about the ninety-nine that did not wander off. [14]In the same way your Father in heaven is not willing that any of these little ones should be lost.

[15]"If your brother sins against you, go and show him his fault, just between the two of you. If he listens to you, you have won your brother over. [16]But if he will not listen, take one or two others along, so that 'every matter may be established by the testimony of two or three witnesses.' [17]If he refuses to listen to them, tell it to the church; and if he refuses to listen even to the church, treat him as you would a pagan or a tax collector.

[18]"I tell you the truth, whatever you bind on earth will be bound in heaven, and whatever you loose on earth will be loosed in heaven.

[19]"Again, I tell you that if two of you on earth agree about anything you ask for, it will be done for you by my Father in heaven. [20]For where two or three come together in my name, there am I with them."

1) What is the point of the parable of the lost sheep? How does the parable relate to what comes before it? How does it relate to what Jesus says next?

2) What is the point of the binding and loosing language? How does this language speak to the problem of one who sins against us?

3) Jesus promises to be with two or three who gather in his name. In context, what seems to be the purpose for their gathering?

Day Four Readings and Questions:

[21]Then Peter came to Jesus and asked, "Lord, how many times shall I forgive my brother when he sins against me? Up to seven times?"

[22]Jesus answered, "I tell you, not seven times, but seventy-seven times.

[23]"Therefore, the kingdom of heaven is like a king who wanted to settle accounts with his servants. [24]As he began the settlement, a man who owed him ten thousand talents was brought to him. [25]Since he was not able to pay, the master ordered that he and his wife and his children and all that he had be sold to repay the debt.

[26]"The servant fell on his knees before him. 'Be patient with me,' he begged, 'and I will pay back everything.' [27]The servant's master took pity on him, canceled the debt and let him go.

[28]"But when that servant went out, he found one of his fellow servants who owed him a hundred denarii. He grabbed him and began to choke him. 'Pay back what you owe me!' he demanded.

[29]"His fellow servant fell to his knees and begged him, 'Be patient with me, and I will pay you back.'

[30]"But he refused. Instead, he went off and had the man thrown into prison until he could pay the debt. [31]When the other servants saw what had happened, they were greatly distressed and went and told their master everything that had happened.

[32]"Then the master called the servant in. 'You wicked servant,' he said, 'I canceled all that debt of yours because you begged me to. [33]Shouldn't you have had mercy on your fellow servant just as I had on you?' [34]In anger his master turned him over to the jailers to be

tortured, until he should pay back all he owed.

³⁵"This is how my heavenly Father will treat each of you unless you forgive your brother from your heart."

1) Does Jesus set a limit on forgiveness in this passage?

2) The TNIV translation says the man owed the king "billions of dollars" while his fellow servant owed him "a few hundred dollars." Why does Jesus use such extreme amounts?

3) Is our forgiveness dependent on forgiving others? If so, is this earning our salvation or "works righteousness"? Why or why not?

Day Five Readings and Questions:

Go back and read the entire passage.

1) What is the connection among children, lost sheep, a brother or sister who sins, and forgiveness?

2) Jesus speaks often in this passage of kings and kingdoms. How does he describe the kingdom of heaven in these verses? How does he describe kings?

3) Does the command to treat the unrepentant brother or sister like a pagan or tax collector contradict Jesus' teaching on forgiveness? How did Jesus treat pagans and tax collectors?

MEDITATIONS ON MATTHEW 17:24-18:35

Jesus is king. This is the message at the very beginning of Matthew. Yet from the beginning, those around Jesus, even his closest disciples, have trouble grasping the nature of this kingdom.

Are we any better at grasping it? Do we associate kingdom with a structure? With rules? With secure borders? Are we too much concerned with who is in or out of the kingdom? Too much concerned with our place in the kingdom?

Jesus reminds us that God's rule trumps the rule of any earthly government. Yes, we voluntarily pay taxes so we will not offend, but we are not mere subjects of the government, we are beloved children of the King of the Universe.

Yet, like Jesus himself, we live our lives as children of the King not in splendor and power, but in service to the weak and powerless. We become little children. What's more we welcome little children. From Jesus we learn to path to greatness, the path of care for little ones, no matter what their age.

To care for these little ones means being careful not to cause them to sin. It means leaving the ninety-nine to risk our lives searching for the lost sheep. It means having the heart of God who forgives without limit.

All this we may be willing to do. However, Jesus says the kingdom of heaven demands that we do what is even more uncomfortable for us. It means lovingly confronting the brother or sister who sins against us. Confronting not to gain revenge or to cause embarrassment to them, but seeking them as a little one and a lost sheep. We confront only to forgive, knowing that God the King himself has canceled our enormous debt. And even if our brother and sister will not listen to our loving words, we treat them as pagans and tax collectors.

And how did Jesus treat pagans and tax collectors? He healed them. He ate with them. He called them to follow. He forgave them.

To live in God's kingdom is to have the gentle heart of God, a heart that forgives. It means experiencing the presence of Jesus with us. If we cannot forgive others, our hearts are closed to God's own forgiveness. That is true tragedy, to miss the kingdom.

"Father, rule in our hearts and lives as King. Fill us with your loving forgiveness so we might forgive those who wrong us. May we know that Jesus is always with us when we forgive."

DEMANDS AND REWARDS

(MATTHEW 19:1-20:34)

Day One Readings and Questions:

¹When Jesus had finished saying these things, he left Galilee and went into the region of Judea to the other side of the Jordan. ²Large crowds followed him, and he healed them there.

³Some Pharisees came to him to test him. They asked, "Is it lawful for a man to divorce his wife for any and every reason?"

⁴"Haven't you read," he replied, "that at the beginning the Creator 'made them male and female,' ⁵and said, 'For this reason a man will leave his father and mother and be united to his wife, and the two will become one flesh'? ⁶So they are no longer two, but one. Therefore what God has joined together, let man not separate."

⁷"Why then," they asked, "did Moses command that a man give his wife a certificate of divorce and send her away?"

⁸Jesus replied, "Moses permitted you to divorce your wives because your hearts were hard. But it was not this way from the beginning. ⁹I tell you that anyone who divorces his wife, except for marital unfaithfulness, and marries another woman commits adultery."

¹⁰The disciples said to him, "If this is the situation between a husband and wife, it is better not to marry."

¹¹Jesus replied, "Not everyone can accept this word, but only those to whom it has been given. ¹²For some are eunuchs because they were born that way; others were made that way by men; and others have renounced marriage because of the kingdom of heaven. The one who can accept this should accept it."

¹³Then little children were brought to Jesus for him to place his hands on them and pray for them. But the disciples rebuked those who brought them.

¹⁴Jesus said, "Let the little children come to me, and do not hinder them, for the kingdom of heaven belongs to such as these." ¹⁵When he had placed his hands on them, he went on from there.

1) How is the question of the Pharisees on divorce a testing of Jesus? Do people still "test" others on the question of divorce?

2) Why do the disciples react the way they to Jesus' teaching on marriage? How did they understand Jesus' teaching on the permanence of marriage?

3) What is the relationship between the section on divorce and the story of Jesus and the children?

Day Two Reading and Questions:

¹⁶Now a man came up to Jesus and asked, "Teacher, what good thing must I do to get eternal life?"

¹⁷"Why do you ask me about what is good?" Jesus replied. "There is only One who is good. If you want to enter life, obey the commandments."

¹⁸"Which ones?" the man inquired.

¹⁹Jesus replied, " 'Do not murder, do not commit adultery, do not steal, do not give false testimony, honor your father and mother,' and 'love your neighbor as yourself.' "

²⁰"All these I have kept," the young man said. "What do I still lack?"

²¹Jesus answered, "If you want to be perfect, go, sell your

possessions and give to the poor, and you will have treasure in heaven. Then come, follow me."

²²When the young man heard this, he went away sad, because he had great wealth.

²³Then Jesus said to his disciples, "I tell you the truth, it is hard for a rich man to enter the kingdom of heaven. ²⁴Again I tell you, it is easier for a camel to go through the eye of a needle than for a rich man to enter the kingdom of God."

²⁵When the disciples heard this, they were greatly astonished and asked, "Who then can be saved?"

²⁶Jesus looked at them and said, "With man this is impossible, but with God all things are possible."

²⁷Peter answered him, "We have left everything to follow you! What then will there be for us?"

²⁸Jesus said to them, "I tell you the truth, at the renewal of all things, when the Son of Man sits on his glorious throne, you who have followed me will also sit on twelve thrones, judging the twelve tribes of Israel. ²⁹And everyone who has left houses or brothers or sisters or father or mother or children or fields for my sake will receive a hundred times as much and will inherit eternal life. ³⁰But many who are first will be last, and many who are last will be first."

1) *Why does Jesus say there is only One who is good? Is Jesus distancing himself from goodness or from God?*

2) *Why does Jesus make such a harsh demand of the rich young man? Does Jesus expect everyone to sell everything and give to the poor? Why not?*

3) *Is Peter right to expect a reward for what he has given up to follow Jesus? Should we serve Jesus to get a reward?*

Day Three Reading and Questions:

¹"For the kingdom of heaven is like a landowner who went out early in the morning to hire men to work in his vineyard. ²He agreed to pay them a denarius for the day and sent them into his vineyard.

³"About the third hour he went out and saw others standing in the marketplace doing nothing. ⁴He told them, 'You also go and work in my vineyard, and I will pay you whatever is right.' ⁵So they went.

⁶"He went out again about the sixth hour and the ninth hour and did the same thing. About the eleventh hour he went out and found still others standing around. He asked them, 'Why have you been standing here all day long doing nothing?'

⁷'Because no one has hired us,' they answered.

"He said to them, 'You also go and work in my vineyard.'

⁸"When evening came, the owner of the vineyard said to his foreman, 'Call the workers and pay them their wages, beginning with the last ones hired and going on to the first.'

⁹"The workers who were hired about the eleventh hour came and each received a denarius. ¹⁰So when those came who were hired first, they expected to receive more. But each one of them also received a denarius. ¹¹When they received it, they began to grumble against the landowner. ¹²'These men who were hired last worked only one hour,' they said, 'and you have made them equal to us who have borne the burden of the work and the heat of the day.'

¹³"But he answered one of them, 'Friend, I am not being unfair to you. Didn't you agree to work for a denarius? ¹⁴Take your pay and go. I want to give the man who was hired last the same as I gave you. ¹⁵Don't I have the right to do what I want with my own money? Or are you envious because I am generous?'

¹⁶"So the last will be first, and the first will be last."

1) *Is the owner of the vineyard fair in his hiring practices? Shouldn't those who worked longer expect better pay than those who worked only one hour?*

2) *Are we ever envious because people are generous? Isn't generosity unfair? Shouldn't we expect God to judge us fairly by treating us all the same?*

3) *Jesus begins and ends this parable by saying, "So the last will be first, and the first will be last" (see 19:30). What does he mean?*

Day Four Reading and Questions:

¹⁷Now as Jesus was going up to Jerusalem, he took the twelve disciples aside and said to them, ¹⁸"We are going up to Jerusalem, and the Son of Man will be betrayed to the chief priests and the teachers of the law. They will condemn him to death ¹⁹and will turn him over to the Gentiles to be mocked and flogged and crucified. On the third day he will be raised to life!"

²⁰Then the mother of Zebedee's sons came to Jesus with her sons and, kneeling down, asked a favor of him.

²¹"What is it you want?" he asked.

She said, "Grant that one of these two sons of mine may sit at your right and the other at your left in your kingdom."

²²"You don't know what you are asking," Jesus said to them. "Can you drink the cup I am going to drink?"

"We can," they answered.

²³Jesus said to them, "You will indeed drink from my cup, but to sit at my right or left is not for me to grant. These places belong to those for whom they have been prepared by my Father."

²⁴When the ten heard about this, they were indignant with the

two brothers. ²⁵Jesus called them together and said, "You know that the rulers of the Gentiles lord it over them, and their high officials exercise authority over them. ²⁶Not so with you. Instead, whoever wants to become great among you must be your servant, ²⁷and whoever wants to be first must be your slave—²⁸just as the Son of Man did not come to be served, but to serve, and to give his life as a ransom for many."

²⁹As Jesus and his disciples were leaving Jericho, a large crowd followed him. ³⁰Two blind men were sitting by the roadside, and when they heard that Jesus was going by, they shouted, "Lord, Son of David, have mercy on us!"

³¹The crowd rebuked them and told them to be quiet, but they shouted all the louder, "Lord, Son of David, have mercy on us!"

³²Jesus stopped and called them. "What do you want me to do for you?" he asked.

³³"Lord," they answered, "we want our sight."

³⁴Jesus had compassion on them and touched their eyes. Immediately they received their sight and followed him.

1) Did Zebedee's sons (James and John) or their mother understand what Jesus said about being crucified? What is the cup he asks them to drink?

2) Why are the ten angry at James and John? What does service have to do with greatness?

3) How does the story of the healing of the blind men relate to what goes before? In what way are the disciples blind to Jesus and his demands?

Day Five Reading and Questions:

Go back and read the entire passage.

1) List what Jesus demands of his disciples and would-be disciples in this passage.

2) List the rewards Jesus promises to disciples and workers in this passage.

3) Do the rewards outweigh the demands? Do the disciples understand the extent of the demands? Do they appreciate the rewards?

MEDITATIONS ON MATTHEW 19:1-20:34

Matthew begins by describing Jesus as a king. He is a benevolent, loving king, but like all kings, he must be obeyed. Indeed, as his disciples, we find he is a demanding Lord.

Jesus demands that a husband be faithful to his wife and a wife to her husband. "Therefore what God has joined together, let not man separate." Such faithfulness is sometimes difficult, so difficult that the disciples decide it is better not to marry. It is better not to marry if one is not willing to keep marriage vows even when the relationship is not all we had hoped.

Jesus demands care for little children. His disciples think him too busy or too important to deal with children. He reminds them and us that we are all children in heaven's kingdom.

Jesus even demands that a rich young man should sell all he has and give to the poor. Is this demand for all disciples? We hope not! Yet the response of the other disciples makes us wonder. They left all for

Jesus. Does he demand any less from us?

Jesus demands that we be as generous as he is himself. As generous as the owner of the vineyard, who pays the one-hour workers the same as the eight-hour workers. He asks us to embrace God's generosity not just for ourselves but for others who (in our minds) have not worked as hard or as long as we have.

Jesus demands that we be servants and slaves to others. He requires us to drink the cup he drinks, the cup of suffering. He calls us to follow him to Jerusalem, to mocking, to flogging, to the cross. He demands we die.

Is Jesus nothing but a demanding Lord? If so, who would follow him? No, he is a loving Savior, sent to seek the lost. He gives his life as a ransom for many. He promises we will rule with him. He promises a hundred times what we have given up. He promises resurrection.

We love and trust those promises. But we must not be blind to the demands of Jesus. Two blind men ask for sight. Jesus gives it. Yet they are not the only ones who are blind. The Pharisees are blind to the purpose of marriage, thinking it is there to please them. When it no longer pleases, they feel free to divorce. Jesus opens their eyes to their hardness of heart. He lets them see the original purpose of God in marriage.

The disciples are blind to the value of children. Jesus opens their eyes. The rich young man is blind to the power money has over him. He refuses to see. The all-day workers are blind to the generosity of the landowner. The disciples cannot see where true greatness resides. Jesus opens their eyes to service.

"Lord Jesus, we want our sight. Open our eyes to the demanding ways of your kingdom. Show us today who we must love, what we must give, and how we must die to live with you."

AUTHORITY

(MATTHEW 21:1-32)

Day One Reading and Questions:

¹As they approached Jerusalem and came to Bethphage on the Mount of Olives, Jesus sent two disciples, ²saying to them, "Go to the village ahead of you, and at once you will find a donkey tied there, with her colt by her. Untie them and bring them to me. ³If anyone says anything to you, tell him that the Lord needs them, and he will send them right away."

⁴This took place to fulfill what was spoken through the prophet:
⁵"Say to the Daughter of Zion,
   'See, your king comes to you,
 gentle and riding on a donkey,
    on a colt, the foal of a donkey.' "

⁶The disciples went and did as Jesus had instructed them. ⁷They brought the donkey and the colt, placed their cloaks on them, and Jesus sat on them. ⁸A very large crowd spread their cloaks on the road, while others cut branches from the trees and spread them on the road. ⁹The crowds that went ahead of him and those that followed shouted,

"Hosanna to the Son of David!"

"Blessed is he who comes in the name of the Lord!"

"Hosanna in the highest!"

¹⁰When Jesus entered Jerusalem, the whole city was stirred and asked, "Who is this?"

¹¹The crowds answered, "This is Jesus, the prophet from Nazareth in Galilee."

1) How does Jesus show he is king in this passage?

2) What do the crowds call Jesus?

3) How else does the crowd recognize the authority of Jesus?

Day Two Reading and Questions:

¹²Jesus entered the temple area and drove out all who were buying and selling there. He overturned the tables of the money changers and the benches of those selling doves. ¹³"It is written," he said to them, " 'My house will be called a house of prayer,' but you are making it a 'den of robbers.' "

¹⁴The blind and the lame came to him at the temple, and he healed them. ¹⁵But when the chief priests and the teachers of the law saw the wonderful things he did and the children shouting in the temple area, "Hosanna to the Son of David," they were indignant.

¹⁶"Do you hear what these children are saying?" they asked him.

"Yes," replied Jesus, "have you never read,

'From the lips of children and infants
you have ordained praise'?"

¹⁷And he left them and went out of the city to Bethany, where he spent the night.

1) Why does Jesus drive out those buying and selling in the temple?

2) After driving them out, what does Jesus do in the temple?

3) Why are the chief priests and teachers of the law indignant? Who has the right to be in the temple?

Day Three Reading and Questions:

[18] Early in the morning, as he was on his way back to the city, he was hungry. [19] Seeing a fig tree by the road, he went up to it but found nothing on it except leaves. Then he said to it, "May you never bear fruit again!" Immediately the tree withered.

[20] When the disciples saw this, they were amazed. "How did the fig tree wither so quickly?" they asked.

[21] Jesus replied, "I tell you the truth, if you have faith and do not doubt, not only can you do what was done to the fig tree, but also you can say to this mountain, 'Go, throw yourself into the sea,' and it will be done. [22] If you believe, you will receive whatever you ask for in prayer."

[23] Jesus entered the temple courts, and, while he was teaching, the chief priests and the elders of the people came to him. "By what authority are you doing these things?" they asked. "And who gave you this authority?"

[24] Jesus replied, "I will also ask you one question. If you answer me, I will tell you by what authority I am doing these things. [25] John's baptism—where did it come from? Was it from heaven, or from men?"

[26] They discussed it among themselves and said, "If we say, 'From heaven,' he will ask, 'Then why didn't you believe him?' But if we say, 'From men'—we are afraid of the people, for they all hold that John was a prophet."

[27] So they answered Jesus, "We don't know."

Then he said, "Neither will I tell you by what authority I am doing these things."

1) Why does Jesus curse the fig tree? What connection is there between the fig tree and the Pharisees and teachers of the law?

2) Why are the chief priests and elders concerned about the authority of Jesus? Where did they get their authority? Where does Jesus get his?

3) Does Jesus answer their question? What is the connection between the authority of John and that of Jesus?

Day Four Reading and Questions:

[28]"What do you think? There was a man who had two sons. He went to the first and said, 'Son, go and work today in the vineyard.'

[29]'I will not,' he answered, but later he changed his mind and went.

[30]"Then the father went to the other son and said the same thing. He answered, 'I will, sir,' but he did not go.

[31]"Which of the two did what his father wanted?"

"The first," they answered.

[32]Jesus said to them, "I tell you the truth, the tax collectors and the prostitutes are entering the kingdom of God ahead of you. For John came to you to show you the way of righteousness, and you did not believe him, but the tax collectors and the prostitutes did. And even after you saw this, you did not repent and believe him."

1) What is the point of the parable? Who is the first son? Who is the second?

2) How does this parable relate to the question of authority?

3) How do you think the chief priests and elders reacted to hearing this parable?

Day Five Reading and Questions:

Go back and read the entire passage.

1) List all the ways Jesus shows power and authority in this passage.

2) What is your first reaction to the word "authority"? Should we question authority? Blindly follow authority? What is a healthy attitude toward authority?

3) When is it right to change ones mind like the first son in the story? What is repentance? How is it shown? How does repentance relate to authority?

MEDITATION ON MATTHEW 21:1-32

"Question Authority!"

It was the cry of my youth. In a world where authorities act violently and unjustly, it's not bad advice.

Yet there is a place for legitimate authority. No matter how we try to convince ourselves that we are absolutely free from authority, we cannot live that way. In particular, we cannot escape the authority of God. What's more, we should not even try to escape it. To live under the authority of God through Christ brings true freedom and happiness.

But what if Jesus demands what we do not want to give? What happens when it is hard, even painful to follow Jesus? That's when obedience to authority is tested.

Who recognizes the authority of Jesus in this passage? A large crowd calls him the son of David and treat him like a king during the triumphal entry. The blind and the lame recognize him. So do the children. Even the fig tree recognizes his power.

Who is blind to Jesus' authority? The chief priests, the teachers of the law, and the elders of the people. In other words, the religious leaders, those who spent their entire lives looking for the authority of God. So why couldn't they see it? Because when it came in the person of Jesus, that authority withered their understanding, their power and position. They had to humbly give control of the temple, of religious teaching, of their own lives to Jesus. They refused to do so.

Are we any better? "Of course we are," you say. "We call Jesus our Lord. We recognize his authority." Do we? Do we make him Lord when he questions all we believe? Are we willing to surrender our desires to his? Will he let him lead us where we do not want to go? Are we willing to work in his vineyard, even though we are his children?

If we ever say "no" to the authority of Jesus, there's only one thing we can do. We must change our mind and go into his vineyard to work. If we ever said "yes" to Jesus (and we all as Christians have made that commitment), we dare not refuse his summons to work. We must live out our recognition of the authority of Jesus each moment of each day.

"Lord Jesus, may we this day make you our Lord, obey your authority, and work in your vineyard, through the power of your Holy Spirit."

INVITATION

(MATTHEW 21:33-22:33)

Day One Reading and Questions:

³³"Listen to another parable: There was a landowner who planted a vineyard. He put a wall around it, dug a winepress in it and built a watchtower. Then he rented the vineyard to some farmers and went away on a journey. ³⁴When the harvest time approached, he sent his servants to the tenants to collect his fruit.

³⁵"The tenants seized his servants; they beat one, killed another, and stoned a third. ³⁶Then he sent other servants to them, more than the first time, and the tenants treated them the same way. ³⁷Last of all, he sent his son to them. 'They will respect my son,' he said.

³⁸"But when the tenants saw the son, they said to each other, 'This is the heir. Come, let's kill him and take his inheritance.' ³⁹So they took him and threw him out of the vineyard and killed him.

⁴⁰"Therefore, when the owner of the vineyard comes, what will he do to those tenants?"

⁴¹"He will bring those wretches to a wretched end," they replied, "and he will rent the vineyard to other tenants, who will give him his share of the crop at harvest time."

⁴²Jesus said to them, "Have you never read in the Scriptures:

'The stone the builders rejected
    has become the capstone;
the Lord has done this,
    and it is marvelous in our eyes'?

⁴³"Therefore I tell you that the kingdom of God will be taken away

from you and given to a people who will produce its fruit. ⁴⁴He who falls on this stone will be broken to pieces, but he on whom it falls will be crushed."

⁴⁵When the chief priests and the Pharisees heard Jesus' parables, they knew he was talking about them. ⁴⁶They looked for a way to arrest him, but they were afraid of the crowd because the people held that he was a prophet.

1) Who is the landowner? Who are the tenants? Who is the son?

2) What is the point of the stone quotation? Who is the stone? Is this stone a helpful thing or a harmful one?

3) How do the chief priests and Pharisees react to Jesus' parables? Why do they react that way? How should they have reacted?

Day Two Reading and Questions:

¹Jesus spoke to them again in parables, saying: ²"The kingdom of heaven is like a king who prepared a wedding banquet for his son. ³He sent his servants to those who had been invited to the banquet to tell them to come, but they refused to come.

⁴"Then he sent some more servants and said, 'Tell those who have been invited that I have prepared my dinner: My oxen and fattened cattle have been butchered, and everything is ready. Come to the wedding banquet.'

⁵"But they paid no attention and went off—one to his field, another to his business. ⁶The rest seized his servants, mistreated them and killed them. ⁷The king was enraged. He sent his army and destroyed those murderers and burned their city.

⁸"Then he said to his servants, 'The wedding banquet is ready, but

those I invited did not deserve to come. ⁹Go to the street corners and invite to the banquet anyone you find.' ¹⁰So the servants went out into the streets and gathered all the people they could find, both good and bad, and the wedding hall was filled with guests.

¹¹"But when the king came in to see the guests, he noticed a man there who was not wearing wedding clothes. ¹²'Friend,' he asked, 'how did you get in here without wedding clothes?' The man was speechless.

¹³"Then the king told the attendants, 'Tie him hand and foot, and throw him outside, into the darkness, where there will be weeping and gnashing of teeth.'

¹⁴"For many are invited, but few are chosen."

1) How does the king react to those who pay no attention to his invitation? Is this an extreme reaction?

2) What is the point of the wedding clothes? Is the man without wedding clothes a victim of circumstances? Should he have known to wear wedding clothes? Why didn't he wear them? Is his punishment just?

3) What is the difference between being invited and being chosen? What separates the invited from the chosen?

Day Three Reading and Questions:

¹⁵Then the Pharisees went out and laid plans to trap him in his words. ¹⁶They sent their disciples to him along with the Herodians. "Teacher," they said, "we know you are a man of integrity and that you teach the way of God in accordance with the truth. You aren't swayed by men, because you pay no attention to who they are. ¹⁷Tell us

then, what is your opinion? Is it right to pay taxes to Caesar or not?"

[18]But Jesus, knowing their evil intent, said, "You hypocrites, why are you trying to trap me? [19]Show me the coin used for paying the tax." They brought him a denarius, [20]and he asked them, "Whose portrait is this? And whose inscription?"

[21]"Caesar's," they replied.

Then he said to them, "Give to Caesar what is Caesar's, and to God what is God's."

[22]When they heard this, they were amazed. So they left him and went away.

1) Do the Pharisees and Herodians tell the truth about Jesus? Do they mean it? If not, why do they say it?

2) How is this a trap for Jesus? What happens if he says "yes"? What happens if he says, "no"? Are most, "Answer yes or no" questions a trap?

3) Why are they amazed at Jesus' answer? What does his answer mean to us today?

Day Four Reading and Questions:

[23]That same day the Sadducees, who say there is no resurrection, came to him with a question. [24]"Teacher," they said, "Moses told us that if a man dies without having children, his brother must marry the widow and have children for him. [25]Now there were seven brothers among us. The first one married and died, and since he had no children, he left his wife to his brother. [26]The same thing happened to the second and third brother, right on down to the seventh. [27]Finally, the woman died. [28]Now then, at the resurrection, whose wife will she be of

the seven, since all of them were married to her?"

²⁹Jesus replied, "You are in error because you do not know the Scriptures or the power of God. ³⁰At the resurrection people will neither marry nor be given in marriage; they will be like the angels in heaven. ³¹But about the resurrection of the dead—have you not read what God said to you, ³²'I am the God of Abraham, the God of Isaac, and the God of Jacob'? He is not the God of the dead but of the living."

³³When the crowds heard this, they were astonished at his teaching.

1) How are the Sadducees ignorant of the Scriptures? What particular Scripture are they ignoring?

2) How are they ignorant of the power of God? Does most speculation about the after-life limit the power of God? How?

3) Although spoken to Moses long after the deaths of Abraham, Isaac, and Jacob, what does the "I am" statement imply about them? Should the Sadducees have understood that passage the way Jesus does?

Day Five Reading and Questions:

Go back and read the entire passage.

1) How are the Pharisees and Sadducees like the tenants? How are they like those invited to the wedding feast?

2) Why do the Pharisees, Herodians, and Sadducees try to trap Jesus? What did they think of Jesus? Can they hear his invitation?

3) *What is the usual reaction to Jesus' teaching in this passage? What is your usual reaction to the teaching of Jesus?*

MEDITATION ON MATTHEW 21:33-22:33

As teachers in a Christian college, my wife Deb and I get several wedding invitations each year. Deb goes to some of the weddings. I go to hardly any. Why? Because all weddings and all receptions look alike after awhile. Students rarely miss me at their weddings, for they have so many friends there. I admit that I rarely regret missing a wedding. I generally open the invitations, think warm thoughts about the couple, and then throw the invitation away.

But what if we missed the greatest wedding of all? The greatest party of all? Often, Jesus compares God's kingdom to a party. Here the invitations go to the usual guest list. All are too busy to come. The king then invites others off the streets. They come but one is thrown out for improper dress. Why? Could he not afford clothes? Were they at the cleaners? No. The story is of God, the just King. This man had responded to the greatest invitation of all, but he responded on his own terms. He will come but he will not show proper respect to the King by wearing wedding clothes. He is invited but not chosen.

We can miss the great party of God's kingdom in two ways. One is by ignoring the invitation. The Pharisees, Herodians, and Sadducees ignore it by trying to trap Jesus instead of graciously accepting what he offers. They, like their ancestors, have killed the messengers of the great landowner. Now they plot to kill even his son. What can the landowner do but destroy them and look for new tenants? What can the king do but extend his invitation to others who will come?

Yes, we know how terrible these Pharisees and Sadducees are. We would never turn down the invitation of God. We want to join the party. But although many are invited, few are chosen. We may think we can come into the presence of God on our own terms. One church recently invited people to commit to the level in which you feel comfortable. But God will not allow us to party in whatever clothes we chose. We must be clothed with Christ himself.

We are invited. The question is, "Will you go to God's party?" Then the question becomes, "Are you willing to dress for it?" How? Only by letting the difficult and amazing teaching of Christ transform us. Only by dying to self and making Jesus Lord. Only then are we chosen.

HYPOCRITES
(MATTHEW 22:34-23:39)

Day One Reading and Questions:

[34]Hearing that Jesus had silenced the Sadducees, the Pharisees got together. [35]One of them, an expert in the law, tested him with this question: [36]"Teacher, which is the greatest commandment in the Law?"

[37]Jesus replied: " 'Love the Lord your God with all your heart and with all your soul and with all your mind.' [38]This is the first and greatest commandment. [39]And the second is like it: 'Love your neighbor as yourself.' [40]All the Law and the Prophets hang on these two commandments."

[41]While the Pharisees were gathered together, Jesus asked them, [42]"What do you think about the Christ? Whose son is he?"

"The son of David," they replied.

[43]He said to them, "How is it then that David, speaking by the Spirit, calls him 'Lord'? For he says,

[44] "'The Lord said to my Lord:
> Sit at my right hand
> until I put your enemies
> under your feet.'

[45]If then David calls him 'Lord,' how can he be his son?" [46]No one could say a word in reply, and from that day on no one dared to ask him any more questions.

1) Why do you think the Pharisees did not respond to the answer of Jesus on the greatest commandment?

2) Why does Jesus turn the tables by asking the Pharisees a question? Why does Jesus continue to bother with the Pharisees?

3) What is the point of the quotation from David? If David calls the Christ, "Lord," what does that imply about the authority of Jesus?

Day Two Readings and Questions:

¹Then Jesus said to the crowds and to his disciples: ²"The teachers of the law and the Pharisees sit in Moses' seat. ³So you must obey them and do everything they tell you. But do not do what they do, for they do not practice what they preach. ⁴They tie up heavy loads and put them on men's shoulders, but they themselves are not willing to lift a finger to move them.

⁵"Everything they do is done for men to see: They make their phylacteries wide and the tassels on their garments long; ⁶they love the place of honor at banquets and the most important seats in the synagogues; ⁷they love to be greeted in the marketplaces and to have men call them 'Rabbi.'

⁸"But you are not to be called 'Rabbi,' for you have only one Master and you are all brothers. ⁹And do not call anyone on earth 'father,' for you have one Father, and he is in heaven. ¹⁰Nor are you to be called 'teacher,' for you have one Teacher, the Christ. ¹¹The greatest among you will be your servant. ¹²For whoever exalts himself will be humbled, and whoever humbles himself will be exalted.

¹³"Woe to you, teachers of the law and Pharisees, you hypocrites! You shut the kingdom of heaven in men's faces. You yourselves do not enter, nor will you let those enter who are trying to.

1) What are some specific examples you can think of when the Pharisees and teachers of the Law did not practice what they preached?

MEDITATIONS

2) Does Jesus literally mean we should never call anyone "Rabbi," "Father," or "Teacher"? What does he mean?

3) How did the teachers of the Law and the Pharisees shut the kingdom in men's faces? Can you think of examples of how religious teachers do the same today?

Day Three Readings and Questions:

[15]"Woe to you, teachers of the law and Pharisees, you hypocrites! You travel over land and sea to win a single convert, and when he becomes one, you make him twice as much a son of hell as you are.

[16]"Woe to you, blind guides! You say, 'If anyone swears by the temple, it means nothing; but if anyone swears by the gold of the temple, he is bound by his oath.' [17]You blind fools! Which is greater: the gold, or the temple that makes the gold sacred? [18]You also say, 'If anyone swears by the altar, it means nothing; but if anyone swears by the gift on it, he is bound by his oath.' [19]You blind men! Which is greater: the gift, or the altar that makes the gift sacred? [20]Therefore, he who swears by the altar swears by it and by everything on it. [21]And he who swears by the temple swears by it and by the one who dwells in it. [22]And he who swears by heaven swears by God's throne and by the one who sits on it.

[23]"Woe to you, teachers of the law and Pharisees, you hypocrites! You give a tenth of your spices—mint, dill and cummin. But you have neglected the more important matters of the law—justice, mercy and faithfulness. You should have practiced the latter, without neglecting the former. [24]You blind guides! You strain out a gnat but swallow a camel.

[25]"Woe to you, teachers of the law and Pharisees, you hypocrites! You clean the outside of the cup and dish, but inside they are full of

greed and self-indulgence. ²⁶Blind Pharisee! First clean the inside of the cup and dish, and then the outside also will be clean.

²⁷"Woe to you, teachers of the law and Pharisees, you hypocrites! You are like whitewashed tombs, which look beautiful on the outside but on the inside are full of dead men's bones and everything unclean. ²⁸In the same way, on the outside you appear to people as righteous but on the inside you are full of hypocrisy and wickedness."

1) Were the teachers of the Law and the Pharisees evangelistic? Is all mission work a good thing? How can it be a bad thing?

2) What was the result of what the teachers of the Law and the Pharisees said about swearing? Was this God's intent in forbidding swearing?

3) What are the teachers of the Law and the Pharisees like on the outside? On the inside?

Day Four Readings and Questions:

²⁹"Woe to you, teachers of the law and Pharisees, you hypocrites! You build tombs for the prophets and decorate the graves of the righteous. ³⁰And you say, 'If we had lived in the days of our forefathers, we would not have taken part with them in shedding the blood of the prophets.' ³¹So you testify against yourselves that you are the descendants of those who murdered the prophets. ³²Fill up, then, the measure of the sin of your forefathers!

³³"You snakes! You brood of vipers! How will you escape being condemned to hell? ³⁴Therefore I am sending you prophets and wise men and teachers. Some of them you will kill and crucify; others you will flog in your synagogues and pursue from town to town. ³⁵And so

upon you will come all the righteous blood that has been shed on earth, from the blood of righteous Abel to the blood of Zechariah son of Berekiah, whom you murdered between the temple and the altar. [36]I tell you the truth, all this will come upon this generation.

[37]"O Jerusalem, Jerusalem, you who kill the prophets and stone those sent to you, how often I have longed to gather your children together, as a hen gathers her chicks under her wings, but you were not willing. [38]Look, your house is left to you desolate. [39]For I tell you, you will not see me again until you say, 'Blessed is he who comes in the name of the Lord.'"

1) *Do the teachers of the Law and the Pharisees feel superior to their ancestors? Why? Do we ever feel spiritually superior to our ancestors? In what ways?*

2) *Why is it particularly bad to kill a prophet or teacher? What will happen to those who kill them?*

3) *Does Jesus want the teachers of the Law and the Pharisees to be lost? Is he happy about their punishment? Why will they be punished?*

Day Five Reading and Questions:

Go back and read the entire passage.

1) *In your own words, describe what it means to be a Pharisee. Do you find some of these characteristics in Christians today? Do you find them in yourself?*

2) *Jesus is gentle toward prostitutes and tax collectors. Why are his words so harsh toward the teachers of the Law and the Pharisees? Is he angry with them? Are these words of love?*

3) Who is the ultimate prophet, wise man, and teacher? What did the teachers of the Law and Pharisees do to him? What does he want to happen to them?

MEDITATION ON MATTHEW 22:34-23:39

Jesus, meek and gentle. Jesus, friend of sinners. Jesus, scourge of the Pharisees.

Why? Why is Jesus so harsh toward the Pharisees and the teachers of the law? He calls them hypocrites. He calls down God's punishment upon them (that's the meaning of "woe to you"). He calls them blind guides and sons of hell. He brands them murderers, blaming them for killing every prophet from Abel to Zechariah.

Why so condemning, Jesus? What happened to the friend of sinners?

Jesus is a friend to the Pharisees and teachers of the law. He wants gently to gather them under his wing. But they are not willing. So to get their attention, to move their cold hearts, he uses strong and forthright language.

I understand the need for the harsh language of Jesus. I myself am a Bible professor ("teacher of the Law") and a recovering Pharisee. I once thought my calling was to set everyone straight. I once was proud of my superior orthodoxy. I once judged others by standards I was not willing to meet.

Jesus had to shout to get my attention. Perhaps I am not alone. Perhaps you too are a recovering Pharisee. If so, then we can appreciate the love behind a strong warning. If my car is stalled on the railroad track, and you gently knock on my window and say, "Did you know the train is coming?" then I should get out of the car and run. But what if I am not willing? What if I refuse to believe you? Then (out of love) you scream and shout, even try to pull me from the car.

But what if I fight you so much you cannot rescue me? Then all that's left is mourning. You so much wanted to save me, but I was not willing.

Such is the case of Jesus and the Pharisees. May it not be the case with us. Being saved begins not with sinning less, but with admitting our need for a savior.

"Lord Jesus, open our blind eyes to see our need for you. Save us from self-deception and hypocrisy. Make us willing to be gathered under your wings."

SIGNS

(MATTHEW 24:1-51)

Day One Reading and Questions:

¹Jesus left the temple and was walking away when his disciples came up to him to call his attention to its buildings. ²"Do you see all these things?" he asked. "I tell you the truth, not one stone here will be left on another; every one will be thrown down."

³As Jesus was sitting on the Mount of Olives, the disciples came to him privately. "Tell us," they said, "when will this happen, and what will be the sign of your coming and of the end of the age?"

⁴Jesus answered: "Watch out that no one deceives you. ⁵For many will come in my name, claiming, 'I am the Christ,' and will deceive many. ⁶You will hear of wars and rumors of wars, but see to it that you are not alarmed. Such things must happen, but the end is still to come. ⁷Nation will rise against nation, and kingdom against kingdom. There will be famines and earthquakes in various places. ⁸All these are the beginning of birth pains.

⁹"Then you will be handed over to be persecuted and put to death, and you will be hated by all nations because of me. ¹⁰At that time many will turn away from the faith and will betray and hate each other, ¹¹and many false prophets will appear and deceive many people. ¹²Because of the increase of wickedness, the love of most will grow cold, ¹³but he who stands firm to the end will be saved. ¹⁴And this gospel of the kingdom will be preached in the whole world as a testimony to all nations, and then the end will come.

MEDITATIONS

1) What question do the disciples ask Jesus? Is this one question or two?

2) Why does talk of the "end times" create so many false Christs and false prophets? What do these false prophets hope to accomplish? Why would people listen to them?

3) Does Jesus paint a picture of a triumphant church in these verses? Explain your answer.

Day Two Reading and Questions:

[15]"So when you see standing in the holy place 'the abomination that causes desolation,' spoken of through the prophet Daniel—let the reader understand—[16]then let those who are in Judea flee to the mountains. [17]Let no one on the roof of his house go down to take anything out of the house. [18]Let no one in the field go back to get his cloak. [19]How dreadful it will be in those days for pregnant women and nursing mothers! [20]Pray that your flight will not take place in winter or on the Sabbath. [21]For then there will be great distress, unequaled from the beginning of the world until now—and never to be equaled again. [22]If those days had not been cut short, no one would survive, but for the sake of the elect those days will be shortened. [23]At that time if anyone says to you, 'Look, here is the Christ!' or, 'There he is!' do not believe it. [24]For false Christs and false prophets will appear and perform great signs and miracles to deceive even the elect—if that were possible. [25]See, I have told you ahead of time.

[26]"So if anyone tells you, 'There he is, out in the desert,' do not go out; or, 'Here he is, in the inner rooms,' do not believe it. [27]For as lightning that comes from the east is visible even in the west, so will be the coming of the Son of Man. [28]Wherever there is a carcass, there the vultures will gather.

1) What visible sign does Jesus mention? What should the followers of Jesus do when they see that sign?

2) Is Jesus talking about the end of the world and final judgment in these verses? If so, how would fleeing to the mountains help? What event is he talking about?

3) What is the point of the lightning statement? Will the coming of Jesus be seen or hidden?

Day Three Reading and Questions:

[29]"Immediately after the distress of those days
   'the sun will be darkened,
      and the moon will not give its light;
   the stars will fall from the sky,
      and the heavenly bodies will be shaken.'
[30]"At that time the sign of the Son of Man will appear in the sky, and all the nations of the earth will mourn. They will see the Son of Man coming on the clouds of the sky, with power and great glory. [31]And he will send his angels with a loud trumpet call, and they will gather his elect from the four winds, from one end of the heavens to the other.

[32]"Now learn this lesson from the fig tree: As soon as its twigs get tender and its leaves come out, you know that summer is near. [33]Even so, when you see all these things, you know that it is near, right at the door. [34]I tell you the truth, this generation will certainly not pass away until all these things have happened. [35]Heaven and earth will pass away, but my words will never pass away.

1) Does this description sound like a great calamity or like the end of the world?

2) *What does one learn from the fig tree? Does Jesus say these events are the end or a sign that the end is near?*

3) *What does Jesus mean when he says, "this generation will certainly not pass away until all these things have happened?" What events were to take place in that generation?"*

Day Four Reading and Questions:

[36]"No one knows about that day or hour, not even the angels in heaven, nor the Son, but only the Father. [37]As it was in the days of Noah, so it will be at the coming of the Son of Man. [38]For in the days before the flood, people were eating and drinking, marrying and giving in marriage, up to the day Noah entered the ark; [39]and they knew nothing about what would happen until the flood came and took them all away. That is how it will be at the coming of the Son of Man. [40]Two men will be in the field; one will be taken and the other left. [41]Two women will be grinding with a hand mill; one will be taken and the other left.

[42]"Therefore keep watch, because you do not know on what day your Lord will come. [43]But understand this: If the owner of the house had known at what time of night the thief was coming, he would have kept watch and would not have let his house be broken into. [44]So you also must be ready, because the Son of Man will come at an hour when you do not expect him.

[45]"Who then is the faithful and wise servant, whom the master has put in charge of the servants in his household to give them their food at the proper time? [46]It will be good for that servant whose master finds him doing so when he returns. [47]I tell you the truth, he will put him in charge of all his possessions. [48]But suppose that servant is wicked and says to himself, 'My master is staying away a long time,'

⁴⁹and he then begins to beat his fellow servants and to eat and drink with drunkards. ⁵⁰The master of that servant will come on a day when he does not expect him and at an hour he is not aware of. ⁵¹He will cut him to pieces and assign him a place with the hypocrites, where there will be weeping and gnashing of teeth."

1) Who alone knows the time of the Second Coming? Since we do not know the time, what should we do?

2) If the master delays his return, what is the servant tempted to do? What's the point of this parable?

3) What does it mean to watch for the Second Coming?

Day Five Reading and Questions:

Go back and read the entire passage.

1) Do you completely understand this passage? Do we have to understand completely to be ready for the Second Coming?

2) Why are people so fascinated by the details of the Second Coming? Why is there so much interest in the Rapture, tribulation, Armageddon, and the signs of the end? Is this interest spiritually healthy?

3) What does Jesus want his disciples to do to be ready for his coming?

MEDITATION ON MATTHEW 24:1-51.

What are the signs of the Second Coming of Christ?

It's a terribly important question. Yet after years of study of this chapter and others like it, I'm not completely sure what Jesus means. Is he talking about the destruction of the temple in Jerusalem in A.D. 70? Is he talking about a future destruction? Is the whole chapter about the Second Coming? Is part of the chapter about what occurs in that generation and part about our future?

I do not have easy answers to these questions and I am suspicious of the easy answers I've heard and read from others. Yet even though I don't completely understand this chapter, there are things here that are clear. No one knows precisely when Christ will return; no one but God himself. Since we do not know, we should be ready.

What does it mean to be ready? Should we try to live each moment of each day with the conscious thought, "The Lord may come today?" I don't think we can. I don't even think we should. But the thought should be there behind our conscious thoughts, informing all that we do.

Many of us know what it's like to wait for a child to be born. The anticipation of our child's birth affects all we do or say or think months before his birth. As time grows closer, we go about our normal business, but always in the back of our minds is "This might be the day." It's the same with the Lord's coming. We know it's soon; we don't know when.

So he encourages us to be ready. We stay ready not by constantly asking, "Will it be today?" but by living lives of quiet obedience, so that whenever he comes, we will be found faithful. We stay ready by doing. We stay ready by remembering his teachings, his miracles, and his life. By reflecting on the real Jesus, the one who astounded his contemporaries, we begin to recognize him. We see him in the lives of those around us, we hear his voice in the words of Scripture, we feel his presence with us in prayer, and we rely on his help when tempted. By following his steps we are being transformed in his image. By walking with him, we are being prepared for that day when we shall see him face to face.

"Lord Jesus, come quickly! Make us ready for your arrival. This day may we be your faithful servants."

JUDGMENT

(MATTHEW 25:1-46)

Day One Reading and Questions:

¹"At that time the kingdom of heaven will be like ten virgins who took their lamps and went out to meet the bridegroom. ²Five of them were foolish and five were wise. ³The foolish ones took their lamps but did not take any oil with them. ⁴The wise, however, took oil in jars along with their lamps. ⁵The bridegroom was a long time in coming, and they all became drowsy and fell asleep.

⁶"At midnight the cry rang out: 'Here's the bridegroom! Come out to meet him!'

⁷"Then all the virgins woke up and trimmed their lamps. ⁸The foolish ones said to the wise, 'Give us some of your oil; our lamps are going out.'

⁹"'No,' they replied, 'there may not be enough for both us and you. Instead, go to those who sell oil and buy some for yourselves.'

¹⁰"But while they were on their way to buy the oil, the bridegroom arrived. The virgins who were ready went in with him to the wedding banquet. And the door was shut.

¹¹"Later the others also came. 'Sir! Sir!' they said. 'Open the door for us!'

¹²"But he replied, 'I tell you the truth, I don't know you.'

¹³"Therefore keep watch, because you do not know the day or the hour."

1) How does this parable relate to the previous chapter on the signs of the coming of Christ?

2) *Why doesn't the groom open the door after it is shut? What does the shutting of the door imply?*

3) *Why don't the wise virgins share with the foolish ones? Does this parable promote selfishness? Are there some things we cannot share with others? Why?*

Day Two Reading and Questions:

[14]"Again, it will be like a man going on a journey, who called his servants and entrusted his property to them. [15]To one he gave five talents of money, to another two talents, and to another one talent, each according to his ability. Then he went on his journey. [16]The man who had received the five talents went at once and put his money to work and gained five more. [17]So also, the one with the two talents gained two more. [18]But the man who had received the one talent went off, dug a hole in the ground and hid his master's money.

[19]"After a long time the master of those servants returned and settled accounts with them. [20]The man who had received the five talents brought the other five. 'Master,' he said, 'you entrusted me with five talents. See, I have gained five more.'

[21]"His master replied, 'Well done, good and faithful servant! You have been faithful with a few things; I will put you in charge of many things. Come and share your master's happiness!'

[22]"The man with the two talents also came. 'Master,' he said, 'you entrusted me with two talents; see, I have gained two more.'

[23]"His master replied, 'Well done, good and faithful servant! You have been faithful with a few things; I will put you in charge of many things. Come and share your master's happiness!'

[24]"Then the man who had received the one talent came. 'Master,' he said, 'I knew that you are a hard man, harvesting where you have

not sown and gathering where you have not scattered seed. ²⁵So I was afraid and went out and hid your talent in the ground. See, here is what belongs to you.'

²⁶"His master replied, 'You wicked, lazy servant! So you knew that I harvest where I have not sown and gather where I have not scattered seed? ²⁷Well then, you should have put my money on deposit with the bankers, so that when I returned I would have received it back with interest.

²⁸" 'Take the talent from him and give it to the one who has the ten talents. ²⁹For everyone who has will be given more, and he will have an abundance. Whoever does not have, even what he has will be taken from him. ³⁰And throw that worthless servant outside, into the darkness, where there will be weeping and gnashing of teeth.' "

1) What did the one-talent servant think about the master? Was he right about him? What emotion ruled the one-talent man?

2) Why does the ten-talent man get an additional talent? Is this just the rich getting richer at the expense of the poor? Why does the man lose his one talent?

3) When does the master return? How does this relate to the last chapter? Why doesn't the master give the servant a second chance?

Day Three Reading and Questions:

³¹"When the Son of Man comes in his glory, and all the angels with him, he will sit on his throne in heavenly glory. ³²All the nations will be gathered before him, and he will separate the people one from another as a shepherd separates the sheep from the goats. ³³He will put the sheep on his right and the goats on his left.

[34]"Then the King will say to those on his right, 'Come, you who are blessed by my Father; take your inheritance, the kingdom prepared for you since the creation of the world. [35]For I was hungry and you gave me something to eat, I was thirsty and you gave me something to drink, I was a stranger and you invited me in, [36]I needed clothes and you clothed me, I was sick and you looked after me, I was in prison and you came to visit me.'

[37]"Then the righteous will answer him, 'Lord, when did we see you hungry and feed you, or thirsty and give you something to drink? [38]When did we see you a stranger and invite you in, or needing clothes and clothe you? [39]When did we see you sick or in prison and go to visit you?'

[40]"The King will reply, 'I tell you the truth, whatever you did for one of the least of these brothers of mine, you did for me.'"

1) Why are those on the right blessed? Did they earn that blessing?

2) Are those on the right surprised by the words of Jesus? Why? Is it possible to serve Jesus and to be unaware of it?

3) Who are "the least of these brothers of mine"? What does Jesus mean by "you did for me"?

Day Four Reading and Questions:

[41]"Then he will say to those on his left, 'Depart from me, you who are cursed, into the eternal fire prepared for the devil and his angels. [42]For I was hungry and you gave me nothing to eat, I was thirsty and you gave me nothing to drink, [43]I was a stranger and you did not invite me in, I needed clothes and you did not clothe me, I was sick and in prison and you did not look after me.'

⁴⁴"They also will answer, 'Lord, when did we see you hungry or thirsty or a stranger or needing clothes or sick or in prison, and did not help you?'

⁴⁵"He will reply, 'I tell you the truth, whatever you did not do for one of the least of these, you did not do for me.'

⁴⁶"Then they will go away to eternal punishment, but the righteous to eternal life."

1) Who is the eternal fire prepared for? What does that tell us about God's plans for humanity?

2) Why is the punishment of those on the left so severe? What had they done to deserve this?

3) Are those on the left surprised at the words of Jesus? Why? What do you think they expected Jesus to say to them?

Day Five Reading and Questions:

Go back and read the entire passage.

1) How is the punishment of the wicked described in these three stories?

2) What is the value of talking of judgment? Is Jesus trying to scare us into obedience?

3) Where do you find grace in these passages?

MEDITATION ON MATTHEW 25:1-46

Judgment day. For years, it was a frightening day to me. Growing up I heard countless sermons vividly picturing the pains of hell. Those sermons scared me not into obedience but into shame.

Perhaps I'm not alone. We all may cringe a bit when we read of darkness, gnashing of teeth, and eternal fire. So why does Jesus, of all people, talk about these things?

Because he loves us. It's hard to see judgment as a sign of love, but that's what it is. God loves us so much that he takes our choices seriously. If we are not ready to enter the wedding banquet, then we cannot. If we think God is a tyrant and we hide our talents, then God will respect that decision. If we ignore those in need, then we are ignoring Jesus. And he will not forever be ignored.

Our God is a God of grace. Jesus is the friend of sinners. But if we hypocritically insist we have a relationship with God when we ignore what he has entrusted to us, we fool only ourselves. If we think we are serving Jesus when we neglect the least of his brothers and sisters, we have forfeited any right to our inheritance as children.

Judgment means life is real and earnest. The consistent picture of judgment in these stories is of those who are inside and those who are outside. Those prepared for the wedding feast are inside enjoying the party. Those who use their talents for the Master are inside, receiving their reward. Those who care for the needy are invited inside to the kingdom prepared for them since the creation. The unprepared, the ones who hide their talents, and those unconcerned for the needy are outside. And the door is shut.

God has prepared a kingdom, a reward, and a banquet for every human being. He invites, he begs, he even becomes human himself to open the door for us. But he will not force us to come in. If we insist on having our own way, he will let us. He will not force his love on us.

How should we react to judgment? Not with fear. Not with shame. But with preparation, work, and service. That's how we open our hearts to the greatest invitation of all.

"Father, prepare our hearts and lives for your judgment. May be always ready for our Master's return, serving those whom he loves."

BETRAYAL

(MATTHEW 26:1-46)

Day One Reading and Questions:

¹When Jesus had finished saying all these things, he said to his disciples, ²"As you know, the Passover is two days away—and the Son of Man will be handed over to be crucified."

³Then the chief priests and the elders of the people assembled in the palace of the high priest, whose name was Caiaphas, ⁴and they plotted to arrest Jesus in some sly way and kill him. ⁵"But not during the Feast," they said, "or there may be a riot among the people."

⁶While Jesus was in Bethany in the home of a man known as Simon the Leper, ⁷a woman came to him with an alabaster jar of very expensive perfume, which she poured on his head as he was reclining at the table.

⁸When the disciples saw this, they were indignant. "Why this waste?" they asked. ⁹"This perfume could have been sold at a high price and the money given to the poor."

¹⁰Aware of this, Jesus said to them, "Why are you bothering this woman? She has done a beautiful thing to me. ¹¹The poor you will always have with you, but you will not always have me. ¹²When she poured this perfume on my body, she did it to prepare me for burial. ¹³I tell you the truth, wherever this gospel is preached throughout the world, what she has done will also be told, in memory of her."

¹⁴Then one of the Twelve—the one called Judas Iscariot—went to the chief priests ¹⁵and asked, "What are you willing to give me if I hand

him over to you?" So they counted out for him thirty silver coins. ¹⁶From then on Judas watched for an opportunity to hand him over.

1) How do the chief priests and elders want to arrest Jesus? Why?

2) "The poor you will always have with you." What does Jesus mean by this? Is he implying that it is not important to care for the poor?

3) What is there in the story of the anointing that prompts Judas to betray Jesus? What motivates Judas?

Day Two Reading and Questions:

¹⁷On the first day of the Feast of Unleavened Bread, the disciples came to Jesus and asked, "Where do you want us to make preparations for you to eat the Passover?"

¹⁸He replied, "Go into the city to a certain man and tell him, 'The Teacher says: My appointed time is near. I am going to celebrate the Passover with my disciples at your house.' " ¹⁹So the disciples did as Jesus had directed them and prepared the Passover.

²⁰When evening came, Jesus was reclining at the table with the Twelve. ²¹And while they were eating, he said, "I tell you the truth, one of you will betray me."

²²They were very sad and began to say to him one after the other, "Surely not I, Lord?"

²³Jesus replied, "The one who has dipped his hand into the bowl with me will betray me. ²⁴The Son of Man will go just as it is written about him. But woe to that man who betrays the Son of Man! It would be better for him if he had not been born."

²⁵Then Judas, the one who would betray him, said, "Surely not I, Rabbi?"

Jesus answered, "Yes, it is you."

[26]While they were eating, Jesus took bread, gave thanks and broke it, and gave it to his disciples, saying, "Take and eat; this is my body."

[27]Then he took the cup, gave thanks and offered it to them, saying, "Drink from it, all of you. [28]This is my blood of the covenant, which is poured out for many for the forgiveness of sins. [29]I tell you, I will not drink of this fruit of the vine from now on until that day when I drink it anew with you in my Father's kingdom."

[30]When they had sung a hymn, they went out to the Mount of Olives.

1) What is the significance of the Passover? What does it celebrate? What is the blood of the covenant?

2) Why does Judas ask, "Is it I?" When Jesus tells him, "Yes, it is you," do the other disciples overhear?

3) What does Jesus mean when he talks about drinking the fruit of the vine in the Father's kingdom?

Day Three Reading and Questions:

[31]Then Jesus told them, "This very night you will all fall away on account of me, for it is written:

'I will strike the shepherd,
 and the sheep of the flock will be scattered.'

[32]But after I have risen, I will go ahead of you into Galilee."

[33]Peter replied, "Even if all fall away on account of you, I never will."

[34]"I tell you the truth," Jesus answered, "this very night, before the rooster crows, you will disown me three times."

³⁵But Peter declared, "Even if I have to die with you, I will never disown you." And all the other disciples said the same.

1) Is Peter's denial as bad as the betrayal by Judas?

2) Why is Peter so sure he will not fall away? How is that a warning to us?

3) Is Peter alone in denying Jesus? What happens to the other disciples when Jesus the shepherd is struck down? Why are the other disciples so sure of their loyalty?

Day Four Reading and Questions:

³⁶Then Jesus went with his disciples to a place called Gethsemane, and he said to them, "Sit here while I go over there and pray." ³⁷He took Peter and the two sons of Zebedee along with him, and he began to be sorrowful and troubled. ³⁸Then he said to them, "My soul is overwhelmed with sorrow to the point of death. Stay here and keep watch with me."

³⁹Going a little farther, he fell with his face to the ground and prayed, "My Father, if it is possible, may this cup be taken from me. Yet not as I will, but as you will."

⁴⁰Then he returned to his disciples and found them sleeping. "Could you men not keep watch with me for one hour?" he asked Peter. ⁴¹"Watch and pray so that you will not fall into temptation. The spirit is willing, but the body is weak."

⁴²He went away a second time and prayed, "My Father, if it is not possible for this cup to be taken away unless I drink it, may your will be done."

⁴³When he came back, he again found them sleeping, because

their eyes were heavy. ⁴⁴So he left them and went away once more and prayed the third time, saying the same thing.

⁴⁵Then he returned to the disciples and said to them, "Are you still sleeping and resting? Look, the hour is near, and the Son of Man is betrayed into the hands of sinners. ⁴⁶Rise, let us go! Here comes my betrayer!"

1) Since Jesus had already predicted his death (see above, Matthew 26:2), why does he pray for the cup to pass? How is the second prayer of Jesus in this passage different from the first prayer?

2) Peter and the disciples had just pledged to die with Jesus. Here they cannot even stay awake and pray. Why the difference between their words and their behavior?

3) What does Jesus say after the third prayer? How has the attitude of Jesus changed? What has Jesus learned in prayer?

Day Five Reading and Questions:

Go back and read the entire passage.

1) Have you even been surprised by the generosity of someone you did not know well? How did that feel? How does Jesus feel about the woman's extravagant gift? How do the disciples feel?

2) Have you even been betrayed or denied by someone close to you? How did that feel? How do you think Jesus felt toward Judas, Peter, and the disciples?

3) Where does Jesus turn when everyone forsakes him? Where should we turn?

MEDITATION ON MATTHEW 26:1-46

Betrayed. Have you even been betrayed? You opened your heart to a friend and he stabbed you in the back. You told her your deepest secrets and she made fun of you to others. Friends. Family. Those we have spent the most time with and helped the most, they sometimes betray us and deny us.

Jesus calls the Twelve. He spends years with them—teaching them, living with them, empowering them. Yet in the moment when he needed them most, they all run away. One takes money to betray him. One denies him three times. The three closest to him cannot even stay awake one hour to pray with him. The sheep all scatter.

Where can we turn when we are betrayed? If we cannot count on those we trusted the most, whom can we count on? Facing betrayal and denial, Jesus goes to his Father. It may seem as though God abandons his Son in the Gethsemane prayer. He does not give him what he asks for. He does not take the cup away. But the Father does listen. And he does give Jesus what he asked for. Jesus prays, "Yet not as I will but as you will." And the loving Father helps Jesus see what he wills. At the end of the third prayer, Jesus is ready for the ordeal that lies before him. "Rise, let us go! Here comes my betrayer!"

What do we do when we are betrayed? Perhaps church leaders have betrayed us. Maybe family members deny they even know us. Perhaps our closest friends wound us. Where can we turn? To a Father who listens to the deepest longings of our hearts. That Father may not give us what we long for, but he does promise to be with us no matter what, as long as it is his will, not our own, that we seek. Where can we turn? To a Savior who knows what it feels like to be betrayed but who still gives his body and blood for us.

But what's worse than being betrayed is to be the betrayer. The disciples are confident in their loyalty, yet all forsake Jesus. Why?

Because they rely on their own strength, not God's. "Watch and pray so that you will not fall into temptation" If we are to be faithful friends of Jesus, we must rely on the power of God to keep us from the temptation to cowardice, self-preservation, denial, and betrayal.

"Lord Jesus, we want to be faithful to you and never to deny you. Father, give us the strength to be loyal, even in the face of betrayal and death."

MEDITATIONS

TRIAL

(MATTHEW 26:47-27:26)

Day One Reading and Questions:

⁴⁷While he was still speaking, Judas, one of the Twelve, arrived. With him was a large crowd armed with swords and clubs, sent from the chief priests and the elders of the people. ⁴⁸Now the betrayer had arranged a signal with them: "The one I kiss is the man; arrest him." ⁴⁹Going at once to Jesus, Judas said, "Greetings, Rabbi!" and kissed him.

⁵⁰Jesus replied, "Friend, do what you came for."

⁵¹Then the men stepped forward, seized Jesus and arrested him. With that, one of Jesus' companions reached for his sword, drew it out and struck the servant of the high priest, cutting off his ear.

⁵²"Put your sword back in its place," Jesus said to him, "for all who draw the sword will die by the sword. ⁵³Do you think I cannot call on my Father, and he will at once put at my disposal more than twelve legions of angels? ⁵⁴But how then would the Scriptures be fulfilled that say it must happen in this way?"

⁵⁵At that time Jesus said to the crowd, "Am I leading a rebellion, that you have come out with swords and clubs to capture me? Every day I sat in the temple courts teaching, and you did not arrest me. ⁵⁶But this has all taken place that the writings of the prophets might be fulfilled." Then all the disciples deserted him and fled.

1) *Why does one of the disciples cut off the servant's ear? Does this act have any relationship to the confidence of the disciples that they would never forsake Jesus?*

2) *Could Jesus have used his power to escape? Why didn't he? How does his refusal to use violent power relate to his statement about the sword?*

3) *Why is the crowd armed with swords and clubs? Had Jesus or his followers shown any violent tendencies before this?*

Day Two Reading and Questions:

⁵⁷Those who had arrested Jesus took him to Caiaphas, the high priest, where the teachers of the law and the elders had assembled. ⁵⁸But Peter followed him at a distance, right up to the courtyard of the high priest. He entered and sat down with the guards to see the outcome.

⁵⁹The chief priests and the whole Sanhedrin were looking for false evidence against Jesus so that they could put him to death. ⁶⁰But they did not find any, though many false witnesses came forward.

⁶¹Finally two came forward and declared, "This fellow said, 'I am able to destroy the temple of God and rebuild it in three days.' "

⁶²Then the high priest stood up and said to Jesus, "Are you not going to answer? What is this testimony that these men are bringing against you?" ⁶³But Jesus remained silent.

The high priest said to him, "I charge you under oath by the living God: Tell us if you are the Christ, the Son of God."

⁶⁴"Yes, it is as you say," Jesus replied. "But I say to all of you: In the future you will see the Son of Man sitting at the right hand of the Mighty One and coming on the clouds of heaven."

⁶⁵Then the high priest tore his clothes and said, "He has spoken blasphemy! Why do we need any more witnesses? Look, now you have heard the blasphemy. ⁶⁶What do you think?"

"He is worthy of death," they answered.

⁶⁷Then they spit in his face and struck him with their fists. Others slapped him ⁶⁸and said, "Prophesy to us, Christ. Who hit you?"

1) Is this a fair trial? Why or why not?

2) What is so wrong about destroying the temple, if one will build it back? How did the chief priests and the Sanhedrin regard the temple? What did Jesus mean by the temple?

3) What did Jesus say that upset the High Priest so much? What does his statement mean?

Day Three Reading and Questions:

⁶⁹Now Peter was sitting out in the courtyard, and a servant girl came to him. "You also were with Jesus of Galilee," she said.
⁷⁰But he denied it before them all. "I don't know what you're talking about," he said.
⁷¹Then he went out to the gateway, where another girl saw him and said to the people there, "This fellow was with Jesus of Nazareth."
⁷²He denied it again, with an oath: "I don't know the man!"
⁷³After a little while, those standing there went up to Peter and said, "Surely you are one of them, for your accent gives you away."
⁷⁴Then he began to call down curses on himself and he swore to them, "I don't know the man!"
⁷⁵Immediately a rooster crowed. Then Peter remembered the word Jesus had spoken: "Before the rooster crows, you will disown me three times." And he went outside and wept bitterly.
¹Early in the morning, all the chief priests and the elders of the people came to the decision to put Jesus to death. ²They bound him, led him away and handed him over to Pilate, the governor.

³When Judas, who had betrayed him, saw that Jesus was condemned, he was seized with remorse and returned the thirty silver coins to the chief priests and the elders. ⁴"I have sinned," he said, "for I have betrayed innocent blood."

"What is that to us?" they replied. "That's your responsibility."

⁵So Judas threw the money into the temple and left. Then he went away and hanged himself.

⁶The chief priests picked up the coins and said, "It is against the law to put this into the treasury, since it is blood money." ⁷So they decided to use the money to buy the potter's field as a burial place for foreigners. ⁸That is why it has been called the Field of Blood to this day. ⁹Then what was spoken by Jeremiah the prophet was fulfilled: "They took the thirty silver coins, the price set on him by the people of Israel, ¹⁰and they used them to buy the potter's field, as the Lord commanded me."

1) Why do Peter's denials become more forceful as he goes along? What is Peter afraid of? What does Peter forget?

2) Is the sin of Judas worse than Peter's? Why is Peter restored to the favor of Jesus and Judas is not?

3) Why won't the priests put the money in the temple treasury? Where did they get the money in the first place? How is this another example of their hypocrisy?

Day Four Reading and Questions:

¹¹Meanwhile Jesus stood before the governor, and the governor asked him, "Are you the king of the Jews?"

"Yes, it is as you say," Jesus replied.

¹²When he was accused by the chief priests and the elders, he gave no answer. ¹³Then Pilate asked him, "Don't you hear the testimony they are bringing against you?" ¹⁴But Jesus made no reply, not even to a single charge—to the great amazement of the governor.

¹⁵Now it was the governor's custom at the Feast to release a prisoner chosen by the crowd. ¹⁶At that time they had a notorious prisoner, called Barabbas. ¹⁷So when the crowd had gathered, Pilate asked them, "Which one do you want me to release to you: Barabbas, or Jesus who is called Christ?" ¹⁸For he knew it was out of envy that they had handed Jesus over to him.

¹⁹While Pilate was sitting on the judge's seat, his wife sent him this message: "Don't have anything to do with that innocent man, for I have suffered a great deal today in a dream because of him."

²⁰But the chief priests and the elders persuaded the crowd to ask for Barabbas and to have Jesus executed.

²¹"Which of the two do you want me to release to you?" asked the governor.

"Barabbas," they answered.

²²"What shall I do, then, with Jesus who is called Christ?" Pilate asked.

They all answered, "Crucify him!"

²³"Why? What crime has he committed?" asked Pilate.

But they shouted all the louder, "Crucify him!"

²⁴When Pilate saw that he was getting nowhere, but that instead an uproar was starting, he took water and washed his hands in front of the crowd. "I am innocent of this man's blood," he said. "It is your responsibility!"

²⁵All the people answered, "Let his blood be on us and on our children!"

²⁶Then he released Barabbas to them. But he had Jesus flogged, and handed him over to be crucified.

1) Why does Jesus not answer the charges against him? Why does that amaze Pilate? What does he say to Pilate's question about being king?

2) Is Pilate innocent of the blood of Jesus? Are the chief priests and elders innocent of his blood? Is the crowd? Are we?

3) According to Pilate, why did the chief priests and elders hand Jesus over to him? Explain.

Day Five Reading and Questions:

Go back and read the entire section.

1) What are the different names or titles given to Jesus in this section? What does each imply?

2) Is the remorse of Judas sincere? What does Judas blame himself for doing? Where does the remorse of Judas go wrong?

3) Do you in any way relate to Barabbas? How?

MEDITATION ON MATTHEW 26:47-27:26

Jesus is King. Matthew makes that clear from the beginning of his gospel. In this section, we see that many misunderstood and rejected his kingship. Some think him a rebel leader with violent followers. They come heavily armed to arrest Jesus. One of Jesus' followers even acts violently, cutting off the ear of the servant of the high priest. In fact, Jesus is king, he has an army of angels, but he chooses not to defend himself. He is the king who wins the battle through losing it.

Jesus is King. As such, he is the Lord of the temple. It is his house. He can destroy it and rebuild it as he sees fit. But the Sanhedrin misunderstands. Jesus is the temple of God. It is his own body that will be destroyed and rebuilt.

Jesus is King. Christ. Messiah. Son of God. Son of Man. This is why the Sanhedrin condemns him. They do not believe he is King; they think him a blasphemer. They are not alone in their lack of faith. Judas loses faith, betrays Jesus, and in despair hangs himself. He cannot recover his faith. Peter loses his faith, denies Jesus three times, but by God's grace reclaims his trust.

Jesus is King. Although Pilate does not believe so. Yet in spite of his unbelief, he condemns Jesus to die on the very charge of being King of the Jews.

Jesus is King. The trial of Jesus is really the trial of those around him. Will they acknowledge him as their King? Or will they betray, deny, and condemn him? We daily face the same trial of our faith.

"King Jesus, may we this day and each day confess you as our King. May we never deny you because of fear. May we follow you even to the cross."

CROSS
(MATTHEW 27:27-61)

Day One Reading and Questions:

²⁷Then the governor's soldiers took Jesus into the Praetorium and gathered the whole company of soldiers around him. ²⁸They stripped him and put a scarlet robe on him, ²⁹and then twisted together a crown of thorns and set it on his head. They put a staff in his right hand and knelt in front of him and mocked him. "Hail, king of the Jews!" they said. ³⁰They spit on him, and took the staff and struck him on the head again and again. ³¹After they had mocked him, they took off the robe and put his own clothes on him. Then they led him away to crucify him.

1) What three symbols of royalty did the soldiers use to mock Jesus?

2) What do you think hurt Jesus the most in this scene?

3) Why did the soldiers mock Jesus? What motivates human beings to do such harm to a stranger?

Day Two Reading and Questions:

³²As they were going out, they met a man from Cyrene, named Simon, and they forced him to carry the cross. ³³They came to a place

called Golgotha (which means The Place of the Skull). ³⁴There they offered Jesus wine to drink, mixed with gall; but after tasting it, he refused to drink it. ³⁵When they had crucified him, they divided up his clothes by casting lots.³⁶And sitting down, they kept watch over him there. ³⁷Above his head they placed the written charge against him: THIS IS JESUS, THE KING OF THE JEWS. ³⁸Two robbers were crucified with him, one on his right and one on his left. ³⁹Those who passed by hurled insults at him, shaking their heads ⁴⁰and saying, "You who are going to destroy the temple and build it in three days, save yourself! Come down from the cross, if you are the Son of God!"

⁴¹In the same way the chief priests, the teachers of the law and the elders mocked him. ⁴²"He saved others," they said, "but he can't save himself! He's the King of Israel! Let him come down now from the cross, and we will believe in him. ⁴³He trusts in God. Let God rescue him now if he wants him, for he said, 'I am the Son of God.' " ⁴⁴In the same way the robbers who were crucified with him also heaped insults on him.

1) Why does Jesus need Simon to carry his cross? Are we forced to carry the cross of Christ?

2) Why does Jesus refuse the wine mixed with gall?

3) What do those around Jesus say to mock him? How does this relate to the charge above his head? Is there irony in how they mock Jesus?

Day Three Reading and Questions:

⁴⁵From the sixth hour until the ninth hour darkness came over all the land. ⁴⁶About the ninth hour Jesus cried out in a loud voice, "Eloi, Eloi, lama sabachthani?"—which means, "My God, my God, why have you forsaken me?"

⁴⁷When some of those standing there heard this, they said, "He's calling Elijah."

⁴⁸Immediately one of them ran and got a sponge. He filled it with wine vinegar, put it on a stick, and offered it to Jesus to drink. ⁴⁹The rest said, "Now leave him alone. Let's see if Elijah comes to save him."

⁵⁰And when Jesus had cried out again in a loud voice, he gave up his spirit.

⁵¹At that moment the curtain of the temple was torn in two from top to bottom. The earth shook and the rocks split. ⁵²The tombs broke open and the bodies of many holy people who had died were raised to life. ⁵³They came out of the tombs, and after Jesus' resurrection they went into the holy city and appeared to many people.

⁵⁴When the centurion and those with him who were guarding Jesus saw the earthquake and all that had happened, they were terrified, and exclaimed, "Surely he was the Son of God!"

⁵⁵Many women were there, watching from a distance. They had followed Jesus from Galilee to care for his needs. ⁵⁶Among them were Mary Magdalene, Mary the mother of James and Joses, and the mother of Zebedee's sons.

1) "My God, my God, why have you forsaken me?" is a quotation from Psalm 22. Read those words in the context of the Psalm. Does the Psalm shed light on the meaning of Jesus on the cross?

2) What is the significance of the tearing of the curtain and the raising of the dead?

3) According to Matthew, who are the only disciples at the cross? Why is this group significant?

Day Four Reading and Questions:

[57] As evening approached, there came a rich man from Arimathea, named Joseph, who had himself become a disciple of Jesus. [58] Going to Pilate, he asked for Jesus' body, and Pilate ordered that it be given to him. [59] Joseph took the body, wrapped it in a clean linen cloth, [60] and placed it in his own new tomb that he had cut out of the rock. He rolled a big stone in front of the entrance to the tomb and went away. [61] Mary Magdalene and the other Mary were sitting there opposite the tomb.

1) How does Joseph show his care for Jesus? Does Joseph remind you of another character in Matthew?

2) What is the significance of rolling the big stone in front of the tomb?

3) What is the significance of the two Mary's being there?

Day Five Reading and Questions:

Go back and read the entire passage.

1) Does this account of the crucifixion strike you as brief? If so, why would Matthew tell the story that way?

2) What are all the ways Jesus is shown to be King in this passage?

3) Who shows the most faith in Jesus in this passage?

MEDITATION ON MATTHEW 27:27-61

Scenes from the cross.

Scene One. Jesus is Mocked. He takes on himself not only the sins of the world, but the shame of the world. The child in the manger, who received gifts befitting a king, now receives a crown. But we see his head, crowned not with a crown of jewels and gold befitting the King of the universe, but crowned with long, sharp, painful thorns. Blood runs down his face, joined by the spit of those who mock him. Blows rain down upon his head. The King is humiliated by us. The King is humiliated for us.

"We adore you, Jesus our King, for by your suffering on the holy cross you have reconciled the world to God."

Scene Two. Jesus is Nailed to the Cross. He cannot carry the cross alone. He knows the experience of having to depend on others. He is offered a drink to ease his pain, but he refuses. He will bear the full weight of the agony. We see the nails driven through his flesh. We see the blood. We see his agony. We feel the hated directed at him by his enemies. We wait with them to watch him die.

"We adore you, Jesus our King, for by your suffering on the holy cross you have reconciled the world to God."

Scene Three. Jesus Dies on the Cross. In agony, he cries, "Why? Why have you forsaken me?" We hear his loud cry. We see him breathe his last breath. His body at last is still, freed from his agony. Yet even in this shameful death, he is shown to be the King. The curtain tears, the tombs open, and the pagan soldier says, "This was the Son of God."

"We adore you, Jesus our King, for by your suffering on the holy cross you have reconciled the world to God."

Scene Four. Jesus is Placed in the Tomb. The King has no place of his own to lay his head, not even in death. But a disciple shows his love by gently wrapping the body and placing it in his tomb. With the women, we see the huge stone rolled across the entrance. Death seems so final. But is it?

"We adore you, Jesus our King, for by your suffering on the holy cross you have reconciled the world to God."

RESURRECTION

(MATTHEW 27:62-28:20)

Day One Reading and Questions:

⁶²The next day, the one after Preparation Day, the chief priests and the Pharisees went to Pilate. ⁶³"Sir," they said, "we remember that while he was still alive that deceiver said, 'After three days I will rise again.' ⁶⁴So give the order for the tomb to be made secure until the third day. Otherwise, his disciples may come and steal the body and tell the people that he has been raised from the dead. This last deception will be worse than the first."

⁶⁵"Take a guard," Pilate answered. "Go, make the tomb as secure as you know how." ⁶⁶So they went and made the tomb secure by putting a seal on the stone and posting the guard.

1) Why do the enemies of Jesus remember his words about resurrection while the disciples seem to forget them?

2) What do the chief priests and the Pharisees say they are afraid of? What are they really afraid of?

3) Why is the sealing and the guarding of the tomb significant?

Day Two Reading and Questions:

¹After the Sabbath, at dawn on the first day of the week, Mary Magdalene and the other Mary went to look at the tomb.

²There was a violent earthquake, for an angel of the Lord came down from heaven and, going to the tomb, rolled back the stone and sat on it. ³His appearance was like lightning, and his clothes were white as snow. ⁴The guards were so afraid of him that they shook and became like dead men.

⁵The angel said to the women, "Do not be afraid, for I know that you are looking for Jesus, who was crucified. ⁶He is not here; he has risen, just as he said. Come and see the place where he lay. ⁷Then go quickly and tell his disciples: 'He has risen from the dead and is going ahead of you into Galilee. There you will see him.' Now I have told you."

⁸So the women hurried away from the tomb, afraid yet filled with joy, and ran to tell his disciples. ⁹Suddenly Jesus met them. "Greetings," he said. They came to him, clasped his feet and worshiped him. ¹⁰Then Jesus said to them, "Do not be afraid. Go and tell my brothers to go to Galilee; there they will see me."

1) *Does Matthew describe the actual resurrection of Jesus? Why not? Does anyone witness the actual resurrection?*

2) *Why are the women both afraid and full of joy? What are they afraid of?*

3) *How do the women react when they meet the resurrected Jesus? Where else in Matthew do we find this reaction to Jesus?*

Day Three Reading and Questions:

[11]While the women were on their way, some of the guards went into the city and reported to the chief priests everything that had happened. [12]When the chief priests had met with the elders and devised a plan, they gave the soldiers a large sum of money, [13]telling them, "You are to say, 'His disciples came during the night and stole him away while we were asleep.' [14]If this report gets to the governor, we will satisfy him and keep you out of trouble." [15]So the soldiers took the money and did as they were instructed. And this story has been widely circulated among the Jews to this very day.

1) *If these are Roman guards, why did they report to the chief priests first? What are the guards afraid of?*

2) *Does the story that the disciples took the body make sense?*

3) *Who else receives money from the chief priests in Matthew?*

Day Four Reading and Questions:

[16]Then the eleven disciples went to Galilee, to the mountain where Jesus had told them to go. [17]When they saw him, they worshiped him; but some doubted. [18]Then Jesus came to them and said, "All authority in heaven and on earth has been given to me. [19]Therefore go and make disciples of all nations, baptizing them in the name of the Father and of the Son and of the Holy Spirit, [20]and teaching them to obey everything I have commanded you. And surely I am with you always, to the very end of the age."

1) What are the two reactions to the resurrected Jesus in this passage? What other examples of those two reactions are found elsewhere in Matthew?

2) Where else in Matthew has Jesus shown his authority?

3) What does it mean to make disciples? Is this different from teaching?

Day Five Reading and Questions:

Go back and read the entire passage.

1) How important is it to believe in the resurrection of Jesus? If Jesus were not raised, would he not still be a great teacher and prophet?

2) How does Jesus act as a king in this passage?

3) Jesus promises to be with his disciples. Was this promise just for those disciples or for all disciples? How is Jesus still with us?

MEDITATION ON MATTHEW 27:62-28:20

Lying in a manger, Jesus has authority. Just ask the Magi who worship him as king. Jesus speaks from the mountain and the people are amazed because he teaches with authority. Jesus says a word and heals a servant. He casts out demons. He raises the dead. He rides into Jerusalem and the crowd proclaims him as their king. He has authority over the temple. He sits in judgment over the nations. He is put to death as King of the Jews.

But his authority is made complete in his resurrection. He has triumphed over death. He is the king who conquers by losing, who lives by dying, who reigns by giving himself for others. This glorious resurrected king gives orders: "Go. Make Disciples. Baptize. Teach."

We must obey the orders of our king. But the power to obey does not come from us alone. We do not go by ourselves. We do not make disciples by our own plans and programs. We do not baptize in our names. We do not teach by our own authority. No. The great and good news that Matthew brings ends with the marvelous words of comfort: "And surely I am with you always, to the very end of the age."

The question we face is "Will we be disciples who worship or will we be those who doubt?" Will we worship King Jesus with all that we have and all that we are, trusting that he is with us every moment? Or will we doubt his authority, his presence, and his love? Worship or doubt? Fear or faith? Present or absent? The good news demands a response.

"King Jesus, we accept your full authority. May we feel your presence with us every hour of every day as we go and make disciples in your name."

A companion volume by the same author

Living God's Love:
An Invitation to Christian Spirituality

176 pages, $12.99 • ISBN 0-9748441-2-8

by Gary Holloway & Earl Lavender

A simple, practical introduction to the classic spiritual disciplines. A wonderful tool for study groups, prayer groups, and classes.

"Our world is hungry for a life-giving way of life. That is what Jesus offered—and offers still. *Living God's Love* makes that way real and alive and accessible to real-world people."

JOHN ORTBERG, AUTHOR OF *THE LIFE YOU'VE ALWAYS WANTED*

"At last: a book that brings the essential subject of spiritual formation down to earth. Clear, reverent, practical, and warm—I'll give this book to people in my church to help them get on a healthy path of authentic Christian living."

BRIAN MCLAREN, AUTHOR OF *A NEW KIND OF CHRISTIAN*

Available through your favorite bookstore
Or call toll free 1·877·634·6004

LEAFWOOD
PUBLISHERS

NOTES

NOTES

NOTES